MW01298235

AIX

Designing Artificial Intelligence

Stanford Edition

BY SUDHA JAMTHE

DEDICATION

Neha, my rock

Figure: One of the 60 self-driving cars piloting in California, driven autonomously by an AI, looking at us on the road as data.

CONTENTS

Introduction to the AI Business   9

Foreword by Tamara McCleary   19

Praise for AIX book   25

CHAPTER 1: AIX: Designing Artificial Intelligence   29

Chapter 2: AI Business Market   33
    2.1 Artificial Intelligence Market Size   33
    2.2 Business Drivers of Diffusion of AI   35
    2.3 AI Business Models   41
    2.4 Artificial Intelligence Business Framework   44

SECTION I: INNOVATE   47

Chapter 3: Data   49
    3.1 Training Data & Learning AI   50
    3.2 4 V's of Data   56
    3.3 Value from data   60

CHAPTER 4: Algorithms   62
    4.1 Machine Learning and Deep Learning   63
    4.2 Facial Recognition   65
    4.3 Computer Vision   71

Chapter 5: The Business Side of AI Models   77
    5.1 Prediction, Clustering & Anomaly Detection   78
    5.2 Machine Learning Data Pipeline   84
    5.3 Recommendation AI Models   89

Chapter 6: AIX Case Studies: AI Modeling for Business Success   95
    6.1 AI Hierarchy of Needs   95
    6.2 Key to Successful AI Modeling in Companies   96

6.3 Managing the Shift in AI Modeling Tools   101

6.4: List of AIX case studies   103

1. Case Study: Blockchain for Energy Consumption   104

2. Case Study: Chatbot for Carrier's Customer Support   107

3. Case Study: AI based Quality Control of Oil Refinery   110

4. Case Study: Digital Transformation of Smart Building   114

5. Case study: McDonald's Personalized Menu at Drive-thru 116

6. Case Study: AI in Healthcare - Listening Out for Us   123

7. Case Study: Omnichannel Personalization for Retail   128

8. Case Study: Low Cost Computer Vision with Arm   137

9. Case Study: Automated Building Management   140

10.Case Study: Retail Ad platform   143

SECTION II: DESIGN   **147**

CHAPTER 7: AIxDesign by Dr. Charles Ikem   **149**

CHAPTER 8: Design Process of AIX   **155**

8.1 Designing for Voice (VUI)   156

8.2 Designing for Machine Learning (MLUX)   165

CHAPTER 9: Designing Shared Spaces   **168**

9.1 Designing Shared In-Car Experience   168

9.2 Learn Shared Space Experience from Buildings   170

9.3 Designing Shared Voice Experience   172

9.4 Shared Devices and Data Bullying   173

SECTION III: PIVOT   **181**

Chapter 10: Automation and Pivoting to AI Jobs   **183**

10.1 Job Market and Reskilling   183

10.2 Pivot your career to AI   186

10.3 Your Role in Automating Jobs in Your Company   192

10.4 AI Product Managers & AI Designers   194

SECTION IV: TRANSFORM   **197**

Chapter 11: TOP AI DISRUPTIONS   **198**

  11.1 Digital Mobility   199

  11.2 Digital Health   199

  11.3 AI for Good   200

Chapter 12: DIGITAL MOBILITY   **201**

  12.1 AI in the Autonomous Vehicle   201

  12.2 Mobility Services   213

  12.3 AI in Retail for Mobility   215

  12.4 Contextual Real-Time Insurance   **216**

Chapter 13: DIGITAL HEALTH   **219**

  13.1 Top AI disruptions in healthcare   221

  13.2 Robotic Haptic Feedback Toys and Robotic Surgery   223

  13.3 Nanobots: Wearables Inside Us   227

    Which AI innovation will disrupt the world?   228

CHAPTER 14: SUSTAINABILITY   **228**

Figure: McKinsey analysis of AI for UN's 17 Sustainability goals 230

SECTION II: IMPACT   **231**

Chapter 15: Autonomous Buildings   **233**

CHAPTER 16: OPEN DATA AND OPEN AI   **247**

  16.1 What is Open AI?   247

  16.2 Federated AI   249

  16.3 Interpretability and Explainable AI   250

CHAPTER 17: AI Ethics   **251**

  17.1 AI Ethics Framework   253

  17.2 Suing an algorithm?   254

  17.3 Inequality & Climate Justice   256

17.3 Morality vs Ethics   260

Chapter 18: Ethical and Smart Automation   265

CHAPTER 19: Conclusion   **268**

Epilogue by Rob Van Kranenburg   **272**

Acknowledgments   **274**

About The Author   **279**

Praise For Sudha Jamthe's IoT Books   **281**

Appendix 1: AI Algorithms for the DataScience Team   **285**

Appendix 2: Best practice mapping data to AI models (from experts on researchgate & quora)   **287**

Appendix 3: List of AIX Case Studies   **290**

Appendix 4: AI Research & References   **291**

Introduction to the AI Business

Artificial Intelligence (AI) business is the power of possibility. The power of AI begins with the power of the computer to crunch large volumes of data and the speed of arriving at an AI model to solve problems for us. This could be predicting a dam failure in a storm or personalizing your next shopping experience with recommendations. That is only the beginning of applying data to your business.

AI is more than automating repetitive jobs. AI gives us the power to redefine our future so that we can imagine new ways of living. AI has begun redefining mobility with connected and self-driving cars for a world of accident free travel. AI has begun redefining healthcare from being reactive to predictive so healthcare in the future is about longer, healthier disease free lives. AI gives us the tools to combat climate change by recreating our world in a sustainable way across a variety of industries.

SUDHA JAMTHE

Data Everywhere is Waiting for You to Power AI

What excites me about AI and the core focus of this book, is the endless possibilities powered by data that takes the shape of many different AI. My research and work has been centered on data from the Internet of Things (IoT) creating a connected, autonomous world, what I refer to as the DriverlessWorld. IoT sensors collect data in the forms of images, sounds, temperature, movement and more. This data can train AI models to solve business problems for cost saving, operational efficiencies or to create new products. The promise of AI has set companies on a digital transformation journey to create value from data locked in many silos within an enterprise. It has begun motivating companies to partner with a larger ecosystem of partners to share data across an industry. For example, banks are collaborating to create AI models that can learn from the collective experience of the industry to prevent fraud. Cities are collaborating by sharing mobility data from e-scooters to plan for multi-modal transportation needs of commuters.

AI is calling upon designers, product managers and business managers to design the right experiences for human computer interaction using data as the foundation. I coined the term "AIX", when referring to this end-to-end AI design process.

What is AIX?

AIX is the end-to-end design of Artificial Intelligence from data to algorithm to the customer experience to solve a business problem.

AIX begins with data and ends with the customer experience. AIX captures the power of the data in the perfect partnership of the machine and human. AIX is focused on solving a specific business problem. For example, AIX is used in Lamborghini cars to allow hands-free voice control of temperature settings during a race. This AIX experience is designed by Alexa Auto using a voice algorithm trained by using sound files of people's conversation.

With Great Power Comes Responsibility

AI with all its power is creating new challenges. AI and the data it powers is impacting the current order of nations, markets and economies. AI is automating some jobs and leading to socio-economic inequalities. This is a huge problem that needs to be thoughtfully addressed by retraining people who will lose their jobs to new AI developments, and giving them the skills they will need to be productive. AI has also woken up nations to the notion of consumer data ownership and consent as a currency to create business value. Europe is regulating the privacy of people's data and self-driving car testing amidst people on the road. This is leading to a rush of AI innovation in the short-term to countries with less regulation. Also, there is a desire to change every job function to become data dependent. This is shifting many non-programmer jobs to use data without any programming knowledge, thereby creating new job roles such as AI Product Management, AI designers and AI Business Development.

AI Industry is in Early Stages

As an author, instructor and technology futurist, I interact with business leaders, entrepreneurs, city leaders and heads of transportation departments on a regular basis. I am routinely involved in planning discussions about digital mobility infrastructure, Autonomous Vehicles and data monetization. I see a common theme across industries globally. We are at the cusp of a strategic inflection point where AI is set to change what it means to be human and how we live our lives and protect our planet. However, the reality today is far from perfect. The way AI is infiltrating our lives today is utter chaos, like a brownian motion of organization. For example, self-driving cars were created as a solution to save lives from traffic accidents. But connected cars and digitizing existing cars with data from connected car parts, driver behavior data and road safety data are creating a cascade of disruption that goes beyond automotive and transportation. They are creating new opportunities in insurance, healthcare, retail and more. For example, insurance companies can use real-time driving patterns to predict the best insurance price for customers to motivate safe driving behaviors.

Data is Waiting in Silos

There is tons of historic data sitting in silos within companies and cities. Additionally there are petabytes of new data being generated in real-time by the minute in factories, cities and hospitals. This covers the gamut of health of people, climate changes in regions and digital twins of equipment. A digital twin is a digital replica of physical assets that companies track using sensors to monitor the health of equipment. For example, airlines track digital twins of airplane parts to predict failure of a part before it happens to proactively repair planes, thereby increasing air travel safety and reducing time saved by making passengers switch planes at the last minute when parts fail while people are waiting to board a plane. Petabytes of this type of data are being collected all around us without us even noticing. This data is promising new business

people, ideas and technology. Multiple camps are arguing abc

ethics and morality. Some people are being opportunistic in us

for making recommendations for movies and ads. Some are

automating factories for cost efficiencies, impacting lives with l

jobs. Some others are creating new AI products such as the

self-driving car, making AI write poetry and art, and innovating

predictive healthcare and sustainable agriculture to create new

ways of living.

Everyone uses data to power the AI but there is no transparency o

what this data is, norhow is it being modeled to create the AI

algorithms. There is currently no standard on how AI interfaces with

voice or computer vision, nor how AI should be designed to create

digital experiences that work with the humans whose lives will be

impacted by AI. Learning AIX will help create standard experiences

for Human-Computer interaction.

AI Disruption Cascades Across Industries

IoT and AI are creating a cascade of disruption. These changes are

not linear changes within one industry. The mobility of data across

an ecosystem holds the promise to create greater value across a city

or the whole industry beyond what is possible by one company or value and more opportunities for innovation. This data can be pictures of people promising to create digital biometric identity using facial recognition or weather data that can predict weather patterns and climate change, or predictive health patterns in a population that can prevent the onset of disease. While this collection of data grows more enormous everyday, businesses are only beginning to scratch the surface of the usefulness of this data and what business value they can create long-term. That is where the promise of AI lies.

Data is Waiting for the AIX Design Experience

Over the past 5 years I have seen multiple IoT, self-driving cars and digitization pilots in companies, cities and hospitals. Each pilot involves the collection of a tremendous amount of data. This data is bursting with value but is waiting for product designers to create people centered experiences that will diffuse AI innovation and create greater customer adoption. This will lead to a cascade of disruption and provide entrepreneurs with nearly unlimited opportunities.

The beauty of data is that it can create new value when it is combined with historic data, or a different kind of value when combined with new data sources. For example, a city can examine historic traffic patterns and better understand the mobility needs of its residents to build new roads where they are most needed. The same city can do better urban planning when combining traffic pattern data with shifts in how people are more environmentally conscious and riding more bicycles. So, looking at data prior to building AI solutions will enable planners to find the gaps that require innovation. Data from cities, businesses and IoT sensors imbedded in wearables and cars provide extremely valuable information about what industries are disrupted and how corporate innovators can manage the upcoming digital transformation. If you are looking to learn how to design new AI solutions with data with a lens on customers, this book is for you.

My research has led me to create a new course at Stanford Continuing Studies Program called "Artificial Intelligence Bootcamp for Product and Business Managers" and this is the companion book for the class.

I have developed an AI business framework for building new businesses in this dynamic space, and for creating new opportunities for companies. I guide my students, the innovators of tomorrow, to apply the business framework to pivot their careers and businesses to unleash data and create the right AIX design experiences to innovate with AI.

people, ideas and technology. Multiple camps are arguing about ethics and morality. Some people are being opportunistic in using AI for making recommendations for movies and ads. Some are automating factories for cost efficiencies, impacting lives with lost jobs. Some others are creating new AI products such as the self-driving car, making AI write poetry and art, and innovating predictive healthcare and sustainable agriculture to create new ways of living.

Everyone uses data to power the AI but there is no transparency on what this data is, norhow is it being modeled to create the AI algorithms. There is currently no standard on how AI interfaces with voice or computer vision, nor how AI should be designed to create digital experiences that work with the humans whose lives will be impacted by AI. Learning AIX will help create standard experiences for Human-Computer interaction.

AI Disruption Cascades Across Industries

IoT and AI are creating a cascade of disruption. These changes are not linear changes within one industry. The mobility of data across an ecosystem holds the promise to create greater value across a city or the whole industry beyond what is possible by one company or organization. For example, self-driving cars were created as a solution to save lives from traffic accidents. But connected cars and digitizing existing cars with data from connected car parts, driver behavior data and road safety data are creating a cascade of disruption that goes beyond automotive and transportation. They are creating new opportunities in insurance, healthcare, retail and more. For example, insurance companies can use real-time driving patterns to predict the best insurance price for customers to motivate safe driving behaviors.

Data is Waiting in Silos

There is tons of historic data sitting in silos within companies and cities. Additionally there are petabytes of new data being generated in real-time by the minute in factories, cities and hospitals. This covers the gamut of health of people, climate changes in regions and digital twins of equipment. A digital twin is a digital replica of physical assets that companies track using sensors to monitor the health of equipment. For example, airlines track digital twins of airplane parts to predict failure of a part before it happens to proactively repair planes, thereby increasing air travel safety and reducing time saved by making passengers switch planes at the last minute when parts fail while people are waiting to board a plane. Petabytes of this type of data are being collected all around us without us even noticing. This data is promising new business historic traffic patterns and better understand the mobility needs of its residents to build new roads where they are most needed. The same city can do better urban planning when combining traffic pattern data with shifts in how people are more environmentally conscious and riding more bicycles. So, looking at data prior to building AI solutions will enable planners to find the gaps that require innovation. Data from cities, businesses and IoT sensors imbedded in wearables and cars provide extremely valuable information about what industries are disrupted and how corporate innovators can manage the upcoming digital transformation. If you are looking to learn how to design new AI solutions with data with a lens on customers, this book is for you.

My research has led me to create a new course at Stanford Continuing Studies Program called "Artificial Intelligence Bootcamp for Product and Business Managers" and this is the companion book for the class.

I have developed an AI business framework for building new businesses in this dynamic space, and for creating new opportunities for companies. I guide my students, the innovators of tomorrow, to apply the business framework to pivot their careers and businesses to unleash data and create the right AIX design experiences to innovate with AI.

value and more opportunities for innovation. This data can be pictures of people promising to create digital biometric identity using facial recognition or weather data that can predict weather patterns and climate change, or predictive health patterns in a population that can prevent the onset of disease. While this collection of data grows more enormous everyday, businesses are only beginning to scratch the surface of the usefulness of this data and what business value they can create long-term. That is where the promise of AI lies.

Data is Waiting for the AIX Design Experience

Over the past 5 years I have seen multiple IoT, self-driving cars and digitization pilots in companies, cities and hospitals. Each pilot involves the collection of a tremendous amount of data. This data is bursting with value but is waiting for product designers to create people centered experiences that will diffuse AI innovation and create greater customer adoption. This will lead to a cascade of disruption and provide entrepreneurs with nearly unlimited opportunities.

The beauty of data is that it can create new value when it is combined with historic data, or a different kind of value when combined with new data sources. For example, a city can examine

In this book, I will tell you about AIX, the end-to-end **design of Artificial Intelligence, starting with data, building the right AI models and then creating the right AIX design experience for people.** Join me, and together we will look at what lies ahead.

As you flip through the pages of this book, visualize the world of inspiration that awaits future generations.

The audience for this book:

- Stanford students from my 'Artificial Intelligence Bootcamp for Product and Business Managers' class who are an inspiration, forever curious and anxious to stake their place in AI Business
- Entrepreneurs, Product Managers and Business Managers, and Technology Strategists looking to fill in the gaps with innovative products and services.
- Anyone interested in moving to the field of AI and want to learn how jobs will shift and what skills they can learn as AI scales mainstream.
- Product Managers, Business Managers, Technology Strategists, Analysts, BPM specialists in Consumer, Enterprise, Smart cities and Industrial settings, looking for ideas and inspiration on how AI will

transform their industries for – Consumer Technology, Automotive, Transportation, Infrastructure, Cities, Retail, Agriculture, Logistics, Healthcare, Oil and Gas, Manufacturing, Energy, Entertainment, Food industry and more.

This is not meant as a book for programmers looking for machine learning code and algorithms as a machine learning researchers or engineers. I explore Machine Learning algorithms that utilize specific data to build AI products and to create business solutions as case studies throughout this book. I have consciously separated the most technical parts using distinct callout boxes. If you are particularly interested in the technical pieces, these callout boxes will provide further references to AI models and practical applications in different business scenarios.

This book is for you as you set out to innovate new entrepreneurial businesses or existing businesses disrupted by Artificial Intelligence. Enjoy and be sure to share your experience with me as you pivot your career and shape the future with your innovations.
- Sudha Jamthe, Technology Futurist, CEO IoTDisruptions.com & Stanford CSP Instructor for Autonomous Vehicles and Artificial Intelligence Courses, @sujamthe, Driverlessworldschool.com

Foreword by Tamara McCleary

Reading this book will change your life. Personally and professionally, as the demarcation between the two has blurred with our 24/7 always-on connected presence, understanding that AIX is the end-to-end design of Artificial Intelligence from data to algorithm to the customer experience may be the key to possessing the power to not only advance in your career, but to being able to pivot and take control of your future in business. To put this in a different context, technology is redefining what it means to be human. If you use a smartphone to communicate by voice, text, and email, manage your calendar, or find immediate answers to questions, you are becoming an augmented human being with your transformative technology (AI) in the palm of your hand always within reach. Resistance is futile, you are being assimilated.

As a futurist and CEO of a technology company, I am surrounded by artificial intelligence and machine learning algorithms that perform social listening and assess copious amounts of data to drive meaningful insights to our B2B and Enterprise clients. I run a global organization harnessing AI and machine learning technologies to effectively lead our company in a successful trajectory. I harness the best from AI today and stay abreast of nascent technologies poised to constantly disrupt how we do business. Likewise, it is incumbent upon today's business leaders, including product and project managers, to ready themselves and their organizations for the future, as I have, by understanding AI and how to harness the power of data and algorithms to not only innovate, but to remain relevant in a rapidly evolving competitive landscape.

I met Sudha Jamthe, in 2016 during my role as an IBM futurist. Sudha was a speaker on a panel I was moderating about unleashing the value of the internet of things [IoT] data with cognitive IoT. Rarely do I meet someone as technically savvy as Sudha who also possesses the ability to translate complex technologies, usually reserved for the expertise of engineers, into actionable insights for the business professional. It was her extraordinary ability to adeptly traverse interdisciplinary domains that sealed our collegiate relationship as we both navigate the uncharted waters of the future, devoting ourselves to mentoring and consulting with practitioners, innovators, Gen Z, and Millennials to senior-level executives, boards, and global organizations about how best to pivot and prepare for the future.

From our digital assistants and vocal interfaces, (think Google Assistant, Siri, Alexa, Cortana, and Watson), to our takeout delivery and pizza ordering apps, to musical suggestions on Spotify, AI is all around us. The most successful businesses of the future will be those that harness the potency of data-fed machine learning algorithms to deliver hyper-personalized and targeted advertising, products and services in real time to customers. In fact, we are entering an era where brands will no longer own the relationship with the customer, but algorithms will own the relationship as we become ever more dependent and reliant upon our digital assistants. Our marketing and sales departments will be marketing and selling to algorithms instead of to humans as machines become the gatekeepers of content offered to individuals.

If you think this is far-fetched, when was the last time you searched for a great restaurant, or ordered something on Amazon because of stellar reviews? We are already offered-up products and services by algorithms that are learning our preferences, and our habits—including our buying behaviors. The genie is out of the bottle and each day we become more assimilated.

AIX begins with data and ends with the customer experience. This is what success in business requires not only for the future, but for the now. Business leaders, product managers and project managers who do not have a thorough working knowledge of how data drives the algorithms and how the algorithms drive customer outcomes will be left behind, unable to pivot in our fast-paced disrupt-or-be-disrupted environment, competing for the attention of our distracted customers who expect us to not only deliver on-promise, but to anticipate their needs.

We don't need leaders with answers, we need leaders with good questions. It's in asking the right questions of the data that we can illuminate the customer's experience by tapping into the answers the machines provide us, in their unique way, through their complex algorithms. We must learn how to ask good questions. Understanding this paradigm shift is what Sudha Jamthe is most known for—her insatiable curiosity paired with an innovative mindset, and a keen aptitude for asking excellent questions.

How will you remain relevant as a business leader, making good decisions, and steering your organization along a successful trajectory? The first step is understanding and applying the wisdom of AIX today. With evolving health technologies and breakthroughs in longevity medicine, we might all expect to live to realize many iterations of our professional careers. The first human being to live to the age of 200 has already been born. What if you had another 100 years to explore what you want to do with your career? It's not what we know but what we're learning that matters most in business and in the world today. This book empowers the business professional, non-engineer, non-programmer to meaningfully engage with IT departments, engineers and product developers to design the future success of business.

May you live long and prosper,

Tamara McCleary, CEO Thulium.co
Futurist and Keynote speaker
February 22, 2020
Boulder, Colorado
TamaraMcCleary.com

Proud of my students: Richard Meyers (left), IoT Project Manager and Richard Schaefer (right), Sr. Enterprise Solutions Manager, Blackberry IoT

Praise for AIX book

"AIX brings together Sudha's deep love and understanding of data with her passion to make it actionable for product and business leaders. AIX is the how-to must-read for humanizing AI from enterprise data." - **Ken Herron, CMO UIB Holdings Pte. Ltd.**

"It's always a great surprise when Sudha Jamthe launches a new book. She has enough expertise to gather information, process it based on her experience, and transform it into knowledge for her students at Stanford University. This book would not be different: Sudha brings the best of both worlds: AI + business. The AIX book is the must-have reference with powerful secrets for success for enterprise AI - the need for business teamwork with technologists to provide the required data in order to build models to unlock great deliverables by designing and training AI algorithms to solve complex business problems." - **Dalton Oliveira, Digital Transformation Advisor, Wardston Consulting.**

"If you are an aspiring entrepreneur looking to innovate in the artificial intelligence space, this book is a must read". – **Natascha Thomson, CEO, MarketingXLerator.**

Sudha is a visionary who can see how AI is connecting the dots of everything from sensors in static buildings to mobile cars, and to the human brain. AIX invites business and product designers to shape the human-computer interface of the future - **Roxy Stimpson, Chief Technology Officer & Enterprise Architect.**

"Jamthe expertly identifies and bridges the gap between the worlds of data science/AI and business management. The surest way to get ahead in your career in the coming years will be to be able to work with AI effectively. For product owners looking to understand and harness the power of data, there's no better guide. AIX will help you put the customer at the heart of your thinking to get the most out of exponential technologies. Easy to read, comprehensive and inspiring, AIX is a uniquely valuable business book." **- David Kerrigan, Author, "The New Acceleration: An Introduction to Artificial Intelligence and the Technologies Making Life Faster."**

"This book "AIX" offers an in-depth guide and case studies for anyone who wants to learn how to build with AI and accelerate digital transformation."- **Josep Clotet, Founding Managing Director, Barcelona Technology School**

"With more and more devices created as connected devices these days, Sudha reminds us with her new book AIX, that data and AI intelligence at the edge are bringing human centered design from Autonomous cars to Autonomous Buildings" - **Ken Sinclair, founder, publisher and owner of AutomatedBuildings.com**

"With AIX, Sudha arms those who understand business, those who understand the customer and those who understand the technology to come together with a pathway to work together to bring the full potential of AI to businesses." - **Patrick Slavenburg, Partner Smartified**

Figure: Barcelona Technology School (BTS) Masters program students, my mentees, and future digital transformation leaders. In the front is Josep Clotet, the GM and visionary of BTS.

CHAPTER 1: AIX: Designing Artificial Intelligence

As the doorbell rings the house is lit with sounds, lights and notifications. The Alexa Echo blinks yellow and updates me on a delivery as the Google Nest Hub announces an arrival. Simultaneously my phone pings with notifications from NestCam security about strangers at my door. They all fight to grab my attention on the same thing.

What is happening in this cacophony of machines in my smart home? Alexa lights up yellow indicating that she has connected to my amazon account and has seen the upcoming deliveries, applying speech to text she listens to my voice and parses out the text using natural language processing and responds with speech. NestCam utilizes computer vision to capture and collect photos of visitors and apply machine learning and facial recognition to identify and notify me of who arrives at my home. What we see here is done everywhere, and isn't limited to our homes. Car companies are collaborating with each other to share data about road safety with an Alexa Auto speaking with us as we drive in some cars. Hospitals use wearable tech to monitor our biometrics and track our health. Meanwhile they have AI chatbots that communicate with various stakeholders that make a hospital run efficiently. As we fly between cities, airports use facial recognition to speed up security checks. From the ground to the air, in a smart city everything is connected.

All of these voice assisted products, security cameras, connected doorbells and invisible intelligence systems are AI-driven. They have learned to make decisions to engage with us at the right time. But, who decides my voice assistant is a female and the delivery robot is a male? Who decides that a blinking yellow light on Alexa will communicate the excitement of receiving a package? Who decides to connect the doorbell to Google Nest hub to allow for a single device that talks to me? And for that matter, how did the camera data come to life and become the human-computer interface for me? What is the secret to designing the AI for me, the human to change my way of living at home, shopping, moving around my city and keeping my life safe, productive, entertained and sustainable?

Welcome to the exciting new world of AIX! As we get ready for a world of AI, you get to design artificial intelligence using data to work for all humanity. You get to pivot your career to design AI in exciting new jobs such as AI product managers, AI Designers and AI business leaders and shape the future. You get to design intelligent business systems that will change how humans live on earth in the future.

Come join me to learn AIX to humanize and genderize the AI, design a customer centered world where we will coexist with the AI. AIX will create the experiences for new interactive interfaces such as Voice, Computer Vision and Augmented Reality.

AI has begun automating life as we know it in its good and bad forms reflecting the biases of our society. Today AI incarcerates some populations unfairly when it impacts a judge's perspective. It targets certain people when offering facial recognition to catch criminals in cities and airports. Today AI models are not open. Several companies are competing to build competing AI models to solve the same problem. This lack of transparency in the data that powers the AI inhibits us from understanding whether the data used to train the AI was biased, making the AI algorithm faulty.

> *"Biased data leads to silos of humans impacted by incorrect AI models. In the end not being open either way fragments humanity and impacts servicing our customers to the full potential of possibilities promised by technology".*

This book on AIX will teach you to train data models tied to your business needs and build products and experiences that are ethical and devoid of bias in training the data.

Welcome to pivoting your career and innovating with AI. Join me on a learning journey to understand the secrets of data, how to choose the right AI algorithm and how to build design experiences for your business innovation opportunity .

Chapter 2: AI Business Market

2.1 Artificial Intelligence Market Size

The Artificial Intelligence market can be defined and sized in two different ways. Technology companies are creating Artificial Intelligence algorithms available in the form of software and cloud platforms. This Artificial Intelligence software market is estimated to reach $118.6 Trillion US Dollars by 2025 according to estimates by the market research firm Tractica.

Businesses across multiple industries use AI algorithms and apply their own data to create AI models that build AI products and solutions. These create operational efficiencies and cost savings and create new products for the enterprise. This business impact of AI can be seen in the growth numbers across multiple industries as they apply AI to improve their business growth. This AI revenue growth is predicted to be USD $14 Trillion by 2035 by Accenture. Accenture research says, "AI has the potential to boost rates of profitability by an average of 38 percent by 2035 and lead to an economic boost of $14 Trillion US dollars across 16 industries in 12 economies by 2035." PwC estimates this AI Business across to be at $14.7 Trillion. This will only happen when AI is designed by a team of professionals of various job roles including product managers, business managers and UX designers that bring out the value of business data. This book aspires to demystify where your business can achieve that productivity and how you can pivot your career to innovate in your company.

Today AI technologies have already begun automating jobs. Look at the figure below from AI Research by Accenture and Frontier Economics showing the promise of the optimization of business processes using AI in multiple industries, promising labor productivity increases by 2035 in select countries. But the promise of AI to impact industries in a global phenomenon waiting for business leaders in every country, in every industry, in every level to pivot to AI to make an impact.

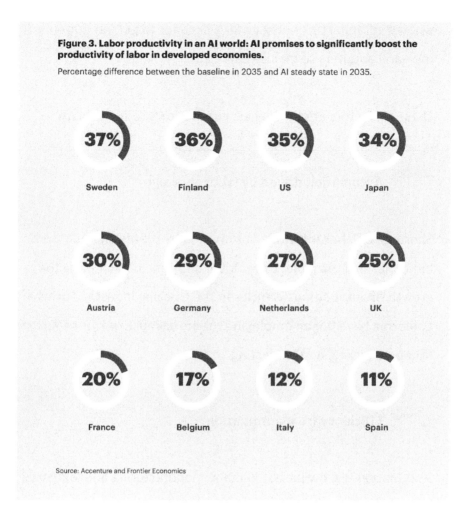

Figure 3. Labor productivity in an AI world: AI promises to significantly boost the productivity of labor in developed economies.

Percentage difference between the baseline in 2035 and AI steady state in 2035.

Source: Accenture and Frontier Economics

Figure: AI Research by Accenture and Frontier Economics

2.2 Business Drivers of Diffusion of AI

AI is getting quickly adopted across every industry and walk of life. The new question is: What is driving this diffusion of innovation when traditional technologies take decades to get integrated from the early adopters to mainstream users?

These six factors are the biggest contributors to AI's growth:

➤ Automation driven by labor shortage

Shortage of labor is inviting automation by robots and AI in some industries. For example, truck driver shortage is prompting the growth of autonomous vehicles in the trucking industry. Farms in California have begun employing robots because of labor shortages for apple picking and harvesting.

➤ Efficiency from automation

Automation is growing fast in many manufacturing and industrial areas where robots are working around the clock and providing higher quality of work.

Figure: Tesla factory builds cars using robots.   Credit: Sudha Jamthe

Robots are now commonplace in car manufacturing. Autonomous tractors and mining equipment are creating efficiencies that are accelerating their adoption. AI has now begun automating some other jobs that require sifting through huge volumes of data. This is in early stages with controversy over whether AI can be trusted to replace human judgment that comes from many years of experience in some job roles. One example of this is HireVue which is interviewing candidates for companies to help them manage huge volumes of job applications, offering to sift through patterns of observed behavior to short-list candidates.

➡ Data sources promising value from data

Companies hold historic data about customers, production schedules, quality assurance and customer service requests. Business leaders are now beginning to understand the power of using company data to train AI models to create an efficiency of cost saving as well as new revenue models. One area not typically talked about is when companies come together to partner using data as their currency. This creates new efficiency as well as a cascading disruption of value chains, all led by date-powered AI. One example of this disruption is the partnership of four automobile brands in Europe that came together to share safety related data collected in real-time from the road. For example, a BMW tire can sense wet road conditions and share this data for other cars behind it to drive safely. These four car brands partnered and built a shared private cloud to store this common data. They made it accessible to other non-car companies such as GPS makers and map companies. This allows other car companies to learn about road conditions,and to help drivers drive safely. The open data from this partnership has the possibility to create AI solutions that can improve the safety on roads in orders of magnitude not conceivable by any one, specific car company.

→ Technology innovations

AI technologies that have been around for decades have been revived with new innovation because of faster CPUs, cheaper storage and a renewed focus on computer vision. Machine learning and deep learning carry out pattern matching utilizing a variety of data from videos from cameras, large customer databases and people talking to voice assistants everywhere.

→ Competition to innovate across countries

Various countries compete with one another to become leaders in AI, and to create algorithmic AI software as a foundational technology for others to use. There is a growing awareness of the need to collaborate between academia and corporations. This stems from the fact that AI needs data and companies have tremendous volumes of data that can be used by academic experts to build AI models. US, China, France, Hong Kong, Switzerland, Japan, UK and Germany lead in terms of collaboration between academia and industry.

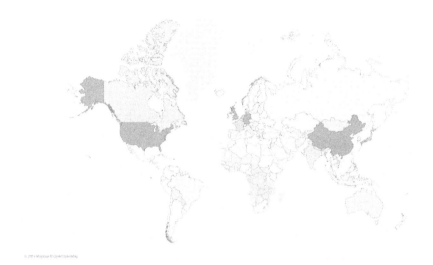

Figure: World Map of Academic-Corporate Collaboration: Total Number of AI papers from AI Index 2019 (Source: Scopus, 2019)

ACAD-CORP Collaboration

1.0   1,000.0

 **Digital transformation**

Business leaders have woken up to the reality that harnessing company data is about adapting change and digital transformation of large companies. The efficiencies created by AI offer cost saving, new revenues and new products and markets that will help companies make the leap into the future. For example, Amazon started as a book seller and retailer but jumpstarted voice assistants in the home and is now bringing voice to the car. Google, Amazon and Apple are reinventing themselves to create new products with AI to create a new future. DeepMind, now part of Google is applying deep learning to predict kidney disease in the UK population using NIH patient data. Omron has added Bluetooth connectivity to its blood pressure monitor to allow users to monitor their daily blood pressure trends using a mobile app.

2.3 AI Business Models

What is going to be the successful business model for artificial intelligence?

AI business models are focused on automating repeatable jobs for cost efficiencies and AI analyzing large volumes of data for decision making for operational efficiency.

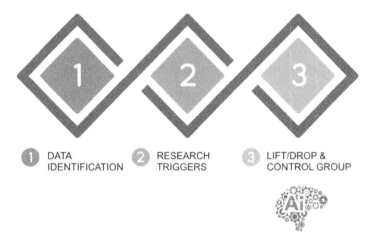

AI model for customer churn

1 DATA IDENTIFICATION
2 RESEARCH TRIGGERS
3 LIFT/DROP & CONTROL GROUP

Figure: AI model for Customer Churn Credit: Sudha Jamthe, model inspired by Tobin Lehman of New North.

The real power of AI lies between the depths of technology and the high level business consideration of the industry. A perfect example is customer churn. A well designed AI algorithm will analyze customer data and help businesses determine where they can improve selection, service and delivery to reduce customer churn. See Figure for AIX for Churn to get from data to AI model. All AI Models should begin with the business goal. Once the business has identified that churn is a problem, the developers can use AIX to

AIX

design algorithms that identify the sources of that churn and opportunities to improve lift.

AI is mostly being implemented inside companies starting with their own engineering and product groups, as can be seen in the report from Figure Eight's State of Machine Learning report and AI below.

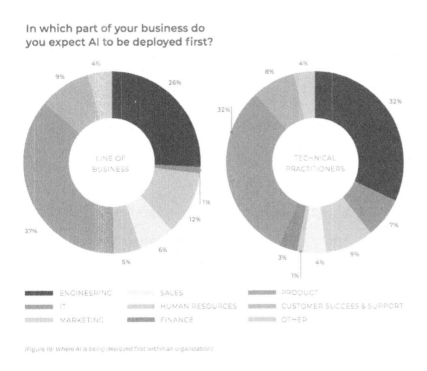

In which part of your business do you expect AI to be deployed first?

(Figure 19. Where AI is being deployed first within an organization)

Figure: What part of business implements AI Source: Figure Eight's State of Machine Learning and AI Report

I believe that this will help businesses develop the data literacy and AI modeling competencies needed as foundation to make effective use of this growing technology in their business. A company with employees who are AI savvy and know the nuances of their own data, will create a cascade of disruption leading to new markets, new products and new solutions from data.

2.4 Artificial Intelligence Business Framework

Artificial Intelligence is set to disrupt multiple industries as we discussed earlier. There is no predetermined path defining exactly how we will transition to the fully connected, autonomous, driverless world. The road is full of opportunities for entrepreneurs, product managers and business innovators to create new businesses and shape the future.

Here is the AI Business Framework that I have developed, and teach my Stanford CSP students.

AIX Design Framework

Business	Data	AI Modeling
Identify Customer Business Problem Value Proposition	Wrangling Labeling Data Engineering	Algorithm Build vs. Buy A/B Testing
Instrumentation	AIxDesign	Strategy
Collect Define Metrics Define Anomaly	Interface AI Persona Data Visualization	Partnerships Cost Structure Revenue Model

(c) Sudha Jamthe use or modify with attribution

Figure: AIX Design Framework by Sudha Jamthe

My AI business framework is a guide for entrepreneurs and corporate innovators to create a new business. It applies to all industries disrupted by AI such as medical, retail, insurance, freight, farming, construction, mining, tourism, medical, logistics, warehouses, new mobility services and more.

The framework starts with the business definition and the problems solved because successful AI in the end always powers the customer. Next comes product management, where the product manager gathers the training data working with AI Engineers. The next step is market development, to iterate until discovering the product market fit. Next comes business model development, to create an ecosystem that shares data as the currency. Also under consideration are opportunities unique to AI, such as creating new business opportunities using data and AI algorithms technologies. AIxdesign is the UX design done with AI which involves designing the user experience by understanding user needs by developing personas, user empathy, user flow maps and testing to arrive at the right design experience that works for the user. AIxDesign takes traditional design processes and iterates using data. Finally, there is the marketing launch strategy and operations to scale the offering. Since AI is always learning, this is a continuous cycle with new data collection, validation of the model and improvement of the AI accuracy over time.

Wishing you success in creating new disruptive AI businesses with the power of data using AIX to design customer centered experiences. Next, we will understand how we innovate with AIX. It begins with understanding data, AI Algorithms and how we develop AI Models with enterprise data.

SECTION I: INNOVATE

What you will learn in this section

1. What is data that trains AI? What are the different forms data takes? What is enterprise data sitting in petabytes of storage in companies? As a business person how you can get the data ready to fine-tune your business to add value to your enterprise.

2. Learn about Algorithms. Get a clear understanding of what Algorithms do and what they can do for your business. How do different Algorithms work to power AI to build products and to create growth opportunities in your business?

3. The final piece is for you to understand the magic of how you can feed data to train algorithms to refine AI Models. What is your role in this as a business or product manager and how can you contribute to the AI models to ensure that they solve your business problem?

Figure: My "Business of self-driving car" class students.

From left to right: Benyue (Emma) Liu, Sr. Product Manager, TigerGraph, Diwakar Bansal, Strategic Marketing Manager, Autonomous Vehicles & Edge Strategy, Intel, Richard Schaefer, Partner & Developer Ecosystems for QNX Car Platform, Blackberry, Sudha Jamthe, Diane McGrath, Strategic Management Consultant, Ajay Dankar, Sr. Director, Adobe Cloud

Chapter 3: Data

What is AIX?

AIX is the end-to-end design of Artificial Intelligence from data to algorithm to AI model to the customer experience to solve a specific business problem.

In this section, you will learn about AI Algorithms and how you can go from your enterprise data and free, open datasets to train AI models to solve business problems. Our goal is to help you, the product and business managers, to understand the foundation of AI models, and your crucial role in bringing your business acumen to fill gaps in data that can train algorithms successfully. You will learn how to use AI Models and data to design the customer experience part in the AIxDesign section later.

3.1 Training Data & Learning AI

Data is the language of AI. Data is what powers the AI. Building AI solutions is an iterative process but it is made of two distinct steps. It is important to understand the difference when you use data to build the AI versus when you use data to communicate with the AI. The first part is done in a lab when building the algorithm. The second part is done with live customers in production, where the AI interacts with the customer in live situations. Both take data as input. The tricky part is that Artificial Intelligence is never completely done and data is what keeps it alive and growing. We call this the "learning AI."

For example, the Nest thermostat is a learning AI. When you buy it, it is just an Internet of Things (IoT) device. It is a thermostat that has internet connectivity so you can control the setting using a mobile app on your phone. The AI is not yet born. As you keep using the Nest, it starts collecting data about what temperature setting is preferable for your home at different times of the day or days of the week. Once it has enough data, Nest becomes a learning thermostat and offers to set your preferred temperature for different times for you. It is still learning because once it sets a temperature, you might not like it and change it manually on any particular day. The Nest takes this information and adapts its AI to learn your preference so that it can offer better predictions next time. This is a continuous learning process and never ends. But at some point it could reach a place where the predicted temperatures work for you and you stop manually adjusting the temperatures.

The Nest team built an AI algorithm in their office, that is standard across all of its devices that is able to predict temperature correctly. They sent it home to your Nest device when you installed the thermostat for the first time. The Nest thermostat adapts this algorithm using your data and builds the right AI model for you. The data you provide by adjusting the Nest manually is the communication you offer it. When you change the setting, you are essentially telling the learning thermostat that you did not like what it recommended and would like the temperature to be this other number instead for this time of the day. That is how data feeds the AI, which allows the device to continue learning..

Another thing to note is that on a cold winter day, you might prefer to increase your temperature inside your home as soon as you come in. This means that the outside weather influences your preferences. So weather becomes another data feed that Nest's learning algorithm could take into consideration to adapt the recommendation of its AI. Your coming in from outside is a factor that is custom to your behavior. Nest also added a motion sensor to the thermostat, to determine whether anyone is home, and offered to allow us to setup profiles for individual people, so it can learn each person's preferences. If it can learn when someone is going to come home on a cold day, it can adjust the temperature prior to arrival. Nest uses this to add another data feed to its learning algorithm, to make the final prediction for the home.

So to summarize, Nest comes with a basic AI algorithm that is capable of predicting preferred temperatures. It then applies your home data and refines the AI Model. Then it integrates with weather data and customer behavior data, about who is in the home and their coming-home patterns. Finally, it makes a temperature prediction, but continues to learn and adapt its AI model as we adjust the temperature manually. Throughout this process, the customer gets a design experience from mobile apps, emails and in this case, the visual design of the Nest thermostat device itself. You as a customer do not stop to think about data or communicating with the AI, let alone training it to work better for you. Customers just interact with the interfaces provided and either like or dislike the experience provided by the AI.

AIX

So, the AIX design journey begins with an algorithm trained with accumulated data, gets refined by additional customer data, and becomes an AI model that makes predictions while offering an experience to solve a customer's problem. Humans have different behavioral expectations from different AI interfaces. Responsibility lies with the product manager and designer to understand the evolving nature of people's interaction with devices and AI, and to design the right customer experience.

Finally, an AI model is here to solve a problem for the customer. Data becomes its enabler and the language that the customer uses to communicate with the AI.

"Digital transformation is not about technology. It is the fundamental reshaping of your business, driven by powerful technologies – and it is relevant for every company, in every sector, everywhere in the world."
- N. Venkat Venkatraman.

Prof. N. Venkat Venkatraman is the David J. McGrath Jr. Professor at Boston University Questrom School of Business. Many years back, he taught me a powerful lesson in my MBA class about digital transformation of businesses using technology. It applies to AI today. We need business leaders to define data that will train the AI for strategic business opportunities. AIX comes with great power, unlike previous technology, as the designer gets to humanize the AI. The customer does not expect to think about data and learning, and can get attached to a human computer interface that offers an engaging experience to solve a problem. For example, people who use Alexa voice assistant think of the device as a female because of the female voice and tone. They slowly begin to engage with the voice assistant like a pet or get attached to it as they become more dependent on the voice assistant. The designer has the power to humanize the device, and genderize it and create a personality, and build trust with the user. You should take this power with responsibility.

Elements of Human Computer Interface

If the AI serves the customer well, then they trust it and give it control to make decisions on their behalf. People want AI to simply work, meaning to get results. If the thermostat does not give the right recommendation, they will lose trust in it. Nest, in fact gives the option to turn off the learning AI setting so that it can still offer the basic value of an IoT thermostat that is set manually and offers remote access to the device.

For most AI, when it fails with bad predictions, people typically lose faith and stop using it. Voice is the one exception. When the voice AI in a car or home does not understand the customer, people typically try to adapt to train the Voice AI. So, the designer and product manager have a lot of power and responsibility to design the user's voice experience to maintain the customer's even when the AI prediction fails some of the time.

We will talk about designing for Voice later in the book.

Designing the experience end of the Nest is a product designer's job, involving the typical design process of understanding their users, their personas, what is the user journey and developing an empathy map to design their experience. The main difference in AIX is that the AI gets designed with data as the input and iterates as it is fed additional data. The AI algorithm then trains the AI model,leading to a design experience that solves a problem and retains the customer's trust.

Next, we will take a deeper look at data and how good, clean data is important to design the AI and how it is a team effort that incorporates the business leader, data scientist, AI engineer, AI designer and product manager.

3.2 4 V's of Data

Enterprise has data from production, maintenance schedules, sales cycles, growth and losses, product launches, customer service data, supply chain data and more. All of this data sits in silos, typically not shared across multiple groups within the company. How do we create value from data by AIX, designing AI models and customer experiences using Artificial Intelligence? It is good to start with a business problem to solve. Sometimes the company has most of the data stored historically over many years. Sometimes it needs to collect more data in real-time by setting up new sensors.

To truly understand the data of an enterprise, it is important to analyse the data through the lens of 4 V's of the data. Refer to the figure below about the 4 V's of data.

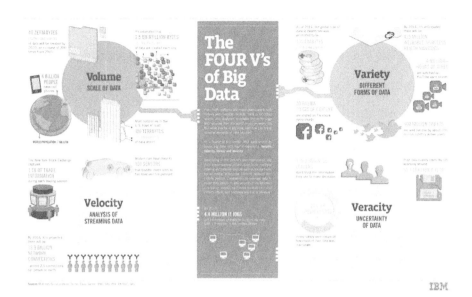

Image credit: IBM

Volume: How much data do we have? Do we have historic data about the customer and various products or items? Since AI learns from training data, lots of data is good to train the AI. Sometimes, the right volume of data needed to train a model for a specific problem might not be obvious until you start working on building the model. **ML optimization** is the gap in training data that needs to be filled for specific business scenarios and requires the product manager or business person to work closely with the AI engineer.

Variety: Are there different forms of data? When you get multiple feeds of data, they come in a variety of forms. Also some of the data could be in the form of numbers, others might be images or sound files. How you organize the data to train the AI algorithm becomes an important consideration because AI algorithms are typically built using one form of data, but a variety of data can inform more insights about the customer.

Velocity: Velocity tracks the real-time nature of the streaming data. Data gains value when it is not mobile, and shared in an ecosystem. For example, weather data can be combined with agricultural yield in precision farming. Weather data can be combined with customer behavioral data to understand retail customer buying propensities. We will look at a case study on this topic later in the book. In summary, data that has a real-time nature has velocity, and it is important to understand the movement of this data in order for your business to succeed as an AI business.

Veracity: How clean is the data? Are we sure about the accuracy of the data? Many Machine Learning AI projects do not proceed past an early pilot stage because the data used is not clean and diverse and hence the AI model ends up with high error rates, or low statistical confidence. "Error rate" defines the statistical confidence of algorithms. For example, say an algorithm that does facial recognition is said to have 75% confidence. This means that the algorithm has a 25% error rate, which means that when you give it a picture of a new person to recognition, it will have a 75% chance to be correct. That means it is wrong 25% of the time. The best way to increase confidence is to retrain the model with more data. Here is where the business people come in. The algorithm needs to be trained with a diverse data set, covering all the business use cases. So for facial recognition, if the customers are Hispanic, add more Hispanic faces. If instead of facial recognition, the algorithm does image recognition of faulty tires, feed more images showing faulty tires in all shades of light or overlapping with other things so that the algorithm can confidently spot a faulty tire to improve quality control using Vision Algorithms.

Unfortunately, it is not clear to everyone that this is a data problem and business users expect the AI model to improve by changing the underlying algorithm. This misperception continues to a frustrating degree in the enterprise across industries today, causing people to question the value and reliability of AI. Business leaders must be taught that the algorithm is not the problem; it just needs more data.

According to the State of AI and Machine Learning report by figure eight, now part of the Appen company, 73% of technical data scientists spend 25% of their time managing, cleaning or labeling data and this makes them unhappy with their jobs.

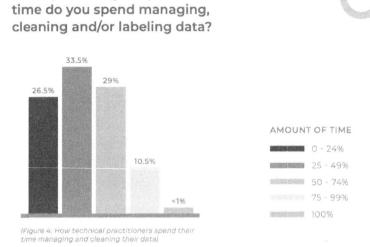

(Figure 4; How technical practitioners spend their time managing and cleaning their data)

Image credit: Figure Eight State of AI And Machine Learning Report 2020.

3.3 Value from data

Data is not the new currency. Data is like money but it needs to move to create money. If it remains static within a company, it is like hiding money under your pillow. It has to flow across departments and among partnerships in an ecosystem.

AIX

AI is about bringing life to data, data that is sitting in silos in many companies and factories, city data about critical infrastructure, healthcare data protected by compliance and consumer behavior data that is spread across multiple locations tied to making life convenient in mobility, retail and entertainment.

The real power of AI is in applying several forms of AI algorithms to model this data, and to form patterns to make decisions to solve real problems. At a fundamental level, all AI does is organize data into patterns, group the data and then make predictions or find anomalies. For example, Google and Facebook use AI to filter out spam.

To harness the power of AI, you need to focus on what problem you want to solve, for whom and how can you design products and services to get the customer to use and to benefit from it.

CHAPTER 4: Algorithms

AI in all its forms is made up of algorithms and data feeds. Algorithms are trained with data and offered as an inference model by companies large and small. This inference model is trained further with real business data feeds by companies until the AI model develops a degree of statistical accuracy that meets the business needs. Many times, more data sources are integrated to create value, not just for one company but for all partners involved.

Technical Explanation of AI:

The foundation of Artificial Intelligence is data and algorithms. Data can be numbers, sound or images and video. A collection of data is known as a dataset. The various attributes of the data are called factors. Think of the factors as columns in a spreadsheet defining a product catalog(e.g. item name, the price of the item, date acquired, number of items left in inventory etc.) Data is used

---

as input to train a statistical model that can discern the shape of the dataset. This model is called an algorithm. The algorithm can look at a new piece of data and make a point prediction.

AI algorithms are designed to make a prediction, also known as a decision or output, about a specific narrowly defined question. For example, a self-driving car uses an algorithm to identify objects on the road. Another algorithm is used to identify traffic lights. Both self-driving car Algorithms are trained using images of scenes on the road showing cars, pedestrians, shrubbery etc.

4.1 Machine Learning and Deep Learning

One way of categorizing AI is about whether the data is structured such as a spreadsheet of numbers or unstructured such as images and sound bites.

Supervised learning is about building an algorithm to make a prediction on large volumes of data when you know what the outcome would be. For example, if we organize two sets of shoes as athletic shoes and dance shoes to show potential customers, we would know when we see an athletic shoe as opposed to dance shoes.. Classification algorithms, using the speed of modern computers, can organize this massive collection of data in ways that would be impossible for humans. Supervised learning is used for structured data.

Unsupervised learning, on the other hand is about building an AI algorithm to make a prediction with a large volume of data where we do not know the factors that contribute to the output. For example, if we want to identify faces of two different persons, we as humans can spot the difference typically. But it is difficult to tell a computer how to identify a face by comparing many attributes or factors such as eyes, nose, cheekbones etc. An unsupervised AI Algorithm can cluster or segment data into groups using unstructured data. As such, we can use an unsupervised algorithm to identify faces or organize customer data into segments when we do not know what factors contribute to such segmentation.

Machine Learning is the most common form of AI used today in 70% of AI applications. Machine learning takes historic data, forms patterns and makes predictions. Machine learning is supervised learning and operates on structured data. Machine learning can be combined with other types of AI to solve problems more efficiently. For example, a business may combine a patient's voice and their medical history in numbers to solve for the urgency to get care.

Deep Learning is an unsupervised learning method of building algorithms that take unstructured data and figure out the factors that matter in making predictions. Deep learning is known for learning rules of games and then challenging humans at playing those games.. Deep learning is also used in facial recognition. Another very promising application is DeepMind, a deep learning algorithm drawing patterns in historic NIH health data of the UK population and predicting kidney disease before it occurs.

4.2 Facial Recognition

AI offers multiple applications based on what type of data is used to train the AI to make predictions. Let us look at Facial Recognition and Computer Vision, both based on images and videos from cameras.

Later on in the book, we will look at applications based on sound and pattern recognition to understand natural language.
The power of facial recognition has knocked at my door. My Nest Cam IQ Outdoor sends me a notification when a stranger stops at my front door. Facial recognition has the power to transform us to tightly integrated connected communities as security cameras scale across our neighborhoods and cities.

I have Nest Cam IQ Outdoors all around my home. Previously, Nest Cam was doing machine learning to identify a human from a cat using image recognition. It now uses facial recognition to recognize faces and gives us the choice to tag people. It then can use anomaly detection to spot people who are not regular visitors and alert us. As connected cameras become more prevalent in our lives and cities, the images and videos will be used for facial recognition to identify people. This will create many opportunities and challenges.

Facial recognition: Consumer applications

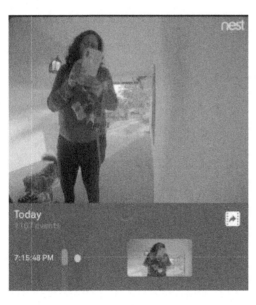

We have facial recognition in our phones and social networks. When Google Photos or Facebook tags pictures of us and maps it to our past pictures, it is training facial recognition algorithms to get better.

Figure: Nest Cam Facial recognition   Source: Sudha Jamthe

My iPhone X uses facial recognition to open my phone. Security cameras in cities use facial recognition software to help law enforcement catch fugitives in real time. They identify people by comparing faces to a criminal database. Facial recognition is used to improve our airport experience from Lufthansa in Los Angeles and Qantas in Sydney. It verifies faces with a central database to speed travel check-ins.

Industrial Application of Facial Recognition

Security Robots

Robots use facial recognition to identify people to provide security to banks and allow customers to check-in within seconds by scanning faces. Security robots patrol corporate campuses and malls in Silicon Valley and could be used to spot intruders.

Drone surveillance

Surveillance drones combine their video footage with body cameras used by the police in America. They use facial recognition to track people without their knowledge. These can protect lives and property, but today there is no transparency on what data is being stored or how it is used.

Figure: Facial recognition   Source: ACLU

The challenge with Facial Recognition: Accuracy and Biases

Amazon offers a facial recognition software called Rekognition that was piloted by the city of Orlando. Orlando discontinued the pilot after Amazon employees protested against the algorithm being inaccurate with biases. Biases are fed into the algorithm when the training data used to improve the algorithm is biased against a certain type of people which might lead to false positives. An ACLU test showed the limitation of Amazon's Rekognition algorithm when it mapped 28 American members of Congress to criminal mugshots and incorrectly identified them as known criminals.

The algorithms that train facial recognition are trained by the data fed to them and are biased in not getting enough coverage of women and people of color. So the facial recognition algorithm is likely to create false positives for these populations. A new startup named Clearview AI is under fire for scrapping people's faces from social networks without their permission to build their facial recognition algorithm and then selling this technology to law enforcement. Ring, the doorbell from Amazon, is also collecting people's faces when they visit homes and building out facial recognition technology called 'Rekognition' and sending it to law enforcement. This takes it one step further in the unethical spectrum because now the doorbell is becoming a surveillance device for communities. Amazon employees objected to its facial recognition AI being used in a pilot in the Dallas airport, claiming it had gaps in its model with biased data. Still, facial recognition as a technology is getting traction. I believe that a technology such a facial recognition that does not work for some segment of population cannot scale long term and will become a liability for the companies and governments who rush to use it without demanding higher accuracy. For example, the facial recognition AI that gives out more false positives to women and people of color will waste the time of law enforcement, cost money and distract law enforcement from spending their resources on capturing the real criminals.

You have the opportunity to understand the potential and opportunity of facial recognition AI technology, and to build this properly for your companies. If you deploy facial recognition as a security check biometric to enter your company, for example, the AI with low confidence will flag and stop many visitors incorrectly. This will disrupt your customers and women working on your premises, so you cannot ignore bias in training data.

The Dallas airport has moved ahead to use facial recognition to scan people at security checks. If the facial recognition stops more women and people of color indiscriminately, it is going to cause delays to all passengers and waste time and money. So apart from the ethics of the situation, this will be a business liability in the long run. Additionally, an inaccurate AI application will make employees lose faith in its accuracy, even if it predicts correctly, and will become a security risk for companies and airports.

Privacy Concerns

Privacy is a huge concern in the U.S. and Europe, as it relates to using such AI software and our data in different situations without our permission. China has taken it a step further and put cameras in schools to watch kids' expressions to see if they appear attentive or bored during a lesson. This is an example where facial recognition can go past identifying faces to combine with machine learning to create new applications. Culture will dictate whether this invades privacy or is embraced by the local communities.

What is possible in the Future with Facial Recognition?

Today, security cameras at homes and airports do facial recognition with the promise to speed up airport check-ins and to keep our homes and offices safe. As a large volume of peoples' faces gets captured, it can be used in ways we are not able to conceive today.

When Nest Cam has enough cameras in a community with well-trained facial recognition data, it can help with the search and rescue of missing kids or track intruders on the run. On the dark side, "eye in the sky" type surveillance could be conducted by AI operating on facial recognition data.

4.3 Computer Vision

Computer Vision looks at images and identifies patterns. For example, an AI can look at a digital copy of blood sample, which is freely available in open datasets, and identify pathogens from regular blood cells. This is used in identifying different strains of flu virus in comparison to previously discovered viruses. Computer vision is used in agriculture to look at sprouting plants to decide which lettuce or strawberry plants are likely to survive and what needs to be weeded out. Computer Vision is the powerful technology behind self-driving cars, cancer identification in hospitals and security cameras which are cropping up in homes, streets and many public spaces.

Clearview AI startup scraped 3 million photos of people from public spaces and social networks and identifies them by their faces. It sells this information to law enforcement, to enable criminal identification, by referencing a central database of criminal faces. 30% of all American faces are believed to be stored on police databases ready for facial recognition by an AI algorithm. We will talk about AI Ethics later in the book, and look at acceptable uses of AI, given the inherent accuracy limitations, when making potentially life threatening decisions.

Imagine you are hungry during a short layover at an airport. What if you could use your phone to ask WhatsApp which restaurant has the shortest line? The security cameras watching the airport terminals know this information. Now, you can talk to the camera via WhatsApp and find information that gets you food or gets you to the restroom with the shortest line. You could even ask a shop to hold the gift you want to buy for your child. You can do this alone or with a group of colleagues who are coming from different terminals. UIB Holdings Pte. Ltd has become one of the early WhatsApp Enterprise Partners, and has integrated UIB's intelligent IoT messaging platform utilizing WhatsApp's Business API. This allows users to chat with devices using WhatsApp and other channels such as voice, text and other messaging apps.

Human-Computer Interface with IoT messaging

Devices talk to us today by sending us notifications on our phones. My phone gets a notification when my Nest Cam security camera notices a person. I cannot talk to the device. I have to open my phone, open the Nest app and click a few times to dig into what the camera saw at that timestamp. This type of human-machine interface is not natural and has a lot of friction for customers to engage. Today, we can talk to voice assistants like Alexa to fetch information from the internet or activate predetermined actions. We need all of our devices to become voice assistants, to offer different services based on their capabilities.

Getting security devices to talk to humans using WhatsApp, UIB now enables messaging with WhatsApp to make devices communicate like voice assistants. For example, Bosch has security cameras for smart offices, warehouses and airports that have been integrated with the UnificationEngine intelligent IoT messaging platform. So now you can use WhatsApp and query security cameras like you would chat with a friend.

Computer Vision with camera   Source: Bosch

Michael Goh, Bosch Building Technology's ASEAN sales director, said, "Bosch's partnership with UIB allows our customers to easily communicate with our connected products through text and natural language. With Unified Inbox and WhatsApp, we query our intelligent cameras' metadata for smart cities and connected building use cases."

Why would you Message a Security Camera?

Chatting with a device using WhatsApp allows us to have a conversation with the device. This opens up creative use cases to query cameras about crowds and updates on what they see on shelves. Imagine a security camera reading car license plates to help locate your car in the garage. Adding WhatsApp messaging to Bosch security cameras using UIB transforms the camera from a passive video streaming device to an interactive conversational personality that you can query in real time.

Business implications of Chatting with Security Cameras

As we get a proliferation of devices all around us in offices, streets and airports, UIB's partnership with WhatsApp allows the devices to be our eyes and ears. On the business side, this opens up new opportunities for airports, brands, real estate properties and smart cities to allow remote conversations with their customers to give them real-time information. It also improves the engagement between businesses and customers using IoT devices.

AIX will bring the power of these devices to us by designing the right end to end experience, from the data training the computerized vision recognition models to the customer experience humanizing the security cameras all around us. Only then will the AI powering these public spaces truly engage in conversations that will benefit the community.

Figure: Sudha Jamthe (left) with my AIX online class student Hani Khalaf, CTO Internet of Things and Digital Cities Solutions Sales from Dubai. Hani is very passionate about the possibilities with Computer Vision.

Chapter 5: The Business Side of AI Models

Are AI Algorithms and AI Models the same or different? The answer is different based on who you ask in the enterprise.

The AI researchers who build the model from raw data say it is the same. The Enterprise AI business managers who end up using generic algorithms such as Logistic Regression to re-train them with their own enterprise data call their final AI inference model as the AI model.

Hani Khalaf, Internet of Things Manager from Dell says *"We take a generic AI algorithm, apply it to "our specific case" and train it on "our own data", then we end up with an AI model."*

5.1 Prediction, Clustering & Anomaly Detection

Ask a business person what they want AI to do. You will not hear about an Algorithm. They are not going to ask for Machine Learning or Deep Learning or Computer Vision. They are going to ask for AI to solve a business problem which leads to three things that all AI can do to solve business problems.

These are:

Prediction: Classification or Regression are supervised learning algorithms that classify data into a line or some shape. With classification, the AI can identify whether data fits in a class and then make predictions about a new data point (e.g classify spam in emails or predict whether a particular cell is a normal cell or a pathogen). With Regression, the output is a continuous quantity. So the prediction can be to forecast a trend (e.g forecasting stock market price by looking at past data). Prediction is also used to offer **recommendations** or offer **personalized choices** to customers. Prediction is the most common form of AI usage in the enterprise across industries. Manufacturing uses prediction for proactive **maintenance schedules** of equipment. Planes check for parts failure before they happen using **Predictive AI.** Marketing uses recommendation engines to predict customer **purchase propensities**. Recommendation engines used in retail are also a form of predictive AI. We will look at recommendation AI in detail later.

Segmenting or Grouping Customers: Clustering groups the data into multiple segments or groups based on some common factors or customer behavior. Segmenting customers is done using clustering algorithms which are unsupervised learning algorithms. This helps to figure out common patterns within each group. These are not obvious patterns that are not obvious to the common eye. Clustering can be used to segment customers to study their backgrounds and behaviors to offer them the best service that fits them. For example, choose a customer segment to decide which ones have the highest chance to engage on a new offer.

Anomaly Detection: An anomaly AI can spot something that is out of ordinary. It could be about discovering a faulty tire in a production line, or alerting the bank on a fraud credit card charge. Fundamentally, anomaly detection can look at data and say whether some metric is not normal or is a misfit or an outlier. Another example is to look at video of seniors in a home to alert healthcare providers if they have had a fall by looking for abnormality in their posture. So it all starts with defining what is considered normal. Also, anomaly is about a specific metric or a bundle of related metrics. So if you want to use anomaly detection for your business, you have to start by defining metrics that you want the Anomaly detection model to look to catch anomalies. This means defining what is normal and what is not normal for each metric.

Look at the figure below. If you are looking for a typical spending level of a user to catch when fraud happens, you can set their average purchase amount as a metric and watch it for anomaly. So if they typically spend $100 in a purchase, a sudden expenditure of $2000 would be an anomaly. It is possible that the user is doing a large travel ticket which is out of ordinary for them. But it is safe for them if the bank flags this an anomaly. My Capital One bank account app flags anomalies for me. I can confirm that it is ok, or ask to hold a purchase when it is not something I bought. This is an example of an end-to-end AIX experience, where the bank runs an anomaly model to solve the business problem of catching fraud transactions but chose to work in partnership with the customer using its app interface. This helps the customer by stopping fraud, but also does not increase the bank's support cost by flagging every odd looking purchase.

Anomaly Detection - Outlier in a data

image credit: Madhav Mishra   #WeeklyWed #live with Sudha Jamthe

Discovering a deviation from the norm related to purchase amount is one form of anomaly detection. An anomaly detection algorithm can also be trained to look at time duration.

For example, if Omron Blood Pressure monitor notices an anomaly in a user's BP it could signal a health problem. But typically a doctor would ask a patient to watch for a period of time to see if the high blood pressure continues before recommending further care. Similarly, in your customer behavior, there could be anomalies in spending levels or engagement, or a change in preferences that can signal an anomaly. It is important to look for a duration of time before concluding that something unusual is an anomaly. For example, if you are looking for customer churn and planning a campaign to offer a discount to bring back inactive customers who were active last year, there might be some customers who are inactive and signal a churn for the duration you are looking at customer data. It is possible that the customer is on vacation or is offline and not using your product or service and will come back on their own.

So it comes down to understanding the insight behind the data, and what is causing the anomaly or change in the pattern. This becomes important to set up in your training data when you build out the AI model for anomaly detection. That is where the business leader's domain knowledge becomes critical. Knowledgeable professionals mustdefine which metrics to watch including the duration of abnormal or anomaly behavior. Otherwise, the AI will send alerts for everything, creating alert fatigue for the user and distracting the business owner from a real problem that is buried in all the noise.

Design Principles for machine learning anomaly detection systems

These are the design considerations for an Anomaly system:

1. **Timeliness:** How quickly does the business want to find an anomaly? Do they want to do this in real-time with streaming data or can they wait for a day or week? This is an important factor that determines what kind of Machine Learning model is used in anomaly detection. For example, they might want to know sudden drop in sales right away so they can take actions to mitigate the root cause.

2. **Scale**: Anomaly is usually metrics for a metric. How many metrics are being tracked becomes important. Some social network systems have billions of metrics tracked. Also the size of the dataset used for the Anomaly detection might be small or larger and determines the resources required to create the model.

3. **Rate of Change**: Is the data changing rapidly or is the system relatively stable?

4. **Conciseness**: Multiple metrics can work together to tell the story of what the anomaly is informing about the business. So conciseness is about deciding we need to track individual metrics or a group of metrics.

5. **Defining what is an anomaly**: Is it possible to define an anomaly ahead of time.

6. **Contextual Analysis:** Whether a supervised or unsupervised model is used depends on the data. If the data is simple

enough to identify what is normal and what is deviant, a supervised learning model could work. Typically semi-supervised models are chosen to allow for feedback loop from user.

5.2 Machine Learning Data Pipeline

The biggest challenge in building out AI Models is the time spent by data scientists in **preparing the data.** Raw data is collected, organized, cleaned and duplicates are removed.

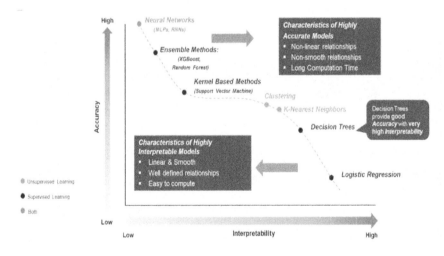

Figure: Accuracy versus Interpretability   Source: DataScience Central

Data optimization is cleaning data by removing noise from data. We do this by removing similar items which are correlated.

Data Wrangling is the transformation of data from 'raw' form to another format that makes it easy for use by analytics and reporting downstream by business users. This happens in large enterprise data which is used by multiple stakeholders for different purposes.

Data Labeling is the biggest problem in data preparation. Data Scientists spend 65% of their time on labelling and preparing the data.

Let us first understand why accurate and appropriate data labelling is critical. If you think of customer data as a spreadsheet, the data is just numbers in rows and columns. If you think about video footage of a security camera guarding our house, every video is made of multiple frames of images and each image is simply a matrix of pixels representing different colors of the image. All of this is just raw numbers to the computer.

Only when we add a label, does the data come to life with a meaning. In Machine Learning, when we want the algorithm to organize the data to find patterns, the labels are the ones that inform us about what factors are grouped together and what factors are contributing to an anomaly in customer behavior. In an image, the labels distinguish one picture from another, differentiating a person from a car, for example. Imagine how crucial this, in terms of object identification, when a self-driving looks at the road.

Feature Engineering is the process of extracting factors from raw data using the business acumen for a specific business. Think of factors like columns in your rows of customer data. Machine learning needs training data to be organized as labelled factors so that the model can organize the data in some pattern to identify the factors that contribute to a certain prediction about the user.

For example, if you are looking at customer churn data, a business person can contribute by adding a factor stating that a particular set of customers visited the company office the previous year and have a higher affinity with the brand. This can help define customers better for the ML model, and train it faster to build a propensity model for a new product offering.

Data Labelling Methods are evolving to save time from labelling data manually. For a Computer Vision model, all video streams have to be marked for various object outlines, for the AI model to learn to identify the different objects. One of the methods to do data labelling is called '**Humans-in-the-loop**." In this method, the labeling is done as a combination of human labeling and the AI model learning patterns and marking objects which are validated or fixed by real people. **Automated labelling** tools use object recognition models on the training data itself to iterate and label all the data after a minimum training.

Active Learning Machine Learning is a form of iterative supervised learning to make the initial model find out what data is valuable from larger unlabeled data. This is useful when you have lots of unlabelled data, and it is very expensive to manually label the data, but there is potential value in the data. For example, a company has 10 years of customer data but the data is not labelled after being merged by many acquisitions over many years. Active Learning refers to the method by which a model gets re-trained by adding more data in phases and examining changes to the model in each round, to determine which data contributes best to improving the model.

Data Curation is the method used to organize data through its lifecycle until storage for future use.

As Business and Product Managers, you need to understand the trade-off between getting huge volumes of data vs. building a generic ML model using the data they have. You should focus on building the optimal Machine Learning pipeline to focus on solving business problems.

If you are passionate about data as the enabler of your business growth, you should focus on the lifecycle of the data downstream, as it flows into other areas of your business, and determine the data strategy that aligns with your business strategy.

This can be done only when the company adopts data in its decision making, and is open to experiment and iterate to find new value from data, by building AI models for a variety of cost saving, revenue generating and strategic business expansions. For example, a bank can look at customer data and apply anomaly detection for fraud prevention. It can use the same data to understand customer usage patterns to reduce support costs and also to build new products to meet the customer life cycle shifts. The starting point should be an intention to serve the customer better and grow their business with a data driven strategy. This will guide the data collection, metrics instrumentation, analysis and potential business cases that can lead to specific AI models that help reach business goals.

5.3 Recommendation AI Models

Recommendation is a special category of algorithms used in three business areas.

1. The most common use of recommendation algorithms is to make recommendations to users to upsell purchases in ecommerce. Xavier Amatriain of Curai.ai, a recommendation algorithm expert from his success with Netflix recommendation, defines a recommendation problem as a utility function that automatically predicts how a user will like an item. So the goal is to figure out what items you should list to ensure that the customer will click and potentially purchase.

2. The not so obvious application of recommendation algorithm is to offer a personalized experience for the user. When you shop online you could get recommendations based on what other users bought that was similar to the item you bought. This is a generic recommendation for

everyone who bought the same item. If the ecommerce site or retailer knows from your past behavior what your preferences are, then they can personalize your experience. In this case the recommendation is made specifically for you and only you. Marketers typically group users into segments and make offers to a group of similar users. Before AI, it was difficult to personalize each user's experience with recommendations catered just to that person. McDonald's recently added personalized menus for people in the drive-through, identifying people by their cars, and tracking them using their license plate. We will cover that personalization case study in-depth with an analysis later in the book.

3. The third and very frequently used recommendation use case is search. The difference is that in search, the query is explicit, while in recommendation options it is implicit. For example, a user might search for "Hawaii" and arrive at a page offering a list of hotel options, or a user logs into an airline site such as Kayak.com looking for air tickets and sees a recommended list of Hawaiian hotel options. The result is the same. In the recommendation, the AI assumes that the user would likely make a purchase if offered a list of

Hawaiian hotels, based on customer behavior, or perhaps on their purchase of an airline ticket to Hawaii.

Data powers all AI and in recommendations it is fully powered customer behavior. Sometimes it is purely based on past customer behavior and sometimes it is combined with real-time data from user engagement on the site. As a product manager, knowing what data feeds the algorithm is critical because it is based solely on historical data. You can run the AI as an inference model developed elsewhere, and it can run on the edge, without Internet connectivity, in a car dashboard. If it is going to require real-time data from customers, then it becomes important to create the AIX experience to collect this data. An example of this is when fashion sites offer the option to do a thumbs up or thumbs down on an offered selection, which they optimize for your next recommended items list. Here, connectivity and the cost of connectivity becomes a business dependency for the success of the recommendation.

Types of Recommendations:

There are many kinds of recommendation algorithms possible. Which one do you need depends on what kind of data is available. Collaborative Filter is based only on user's behavior. So they show items based on what the user previously searched or liked or bought. In this case, there is no value to the domain expertise whether the recommendation is for cars or movies or hotels in Hawaii. Within collaborative filtering, it can be user-based or item-based. Both are agnostic to actual items. For example, "People who bought this also bought.." on Amazon leverages the relationship between users. Item-based lists show items based on the similarity to items identified from the user's past behavior, as opposed to the attributes of the items. On the other hand, content based recommendation is based only on domain knowledge derived from items, not on user behavior. Social recommendations leverage connections between users. A hybrid recommendation approach combines all of the above.

As a business person, it is important to know what your business goal is and what data assets you have to leverage the best recommendation approach as your solution.

It is easy to assume that all ecommerce is about conversion and increased sales. It becomes a business decision when you have to determine whether you have the potential to increase sales by offering an item using this content-based recommendation strategy. One consideration might be the availability of domain knowledge when you expand your business to a new category. Or, whether you have enough past customer purchase data when you expand to new markets. Or you might make a strategic decision to expand purchases by the same customer into multiple categories of items, instead of offering the same category item to the same customer.

The good news is that the AI model can sift through the customer data and arrive at a model that you can test to meet your business goals.

In summary, remember that the technologist or Machine Learning researcher is thinking about what algorithm to use and how to improve the algorithm's performance, to get a higher degree of statistical confidence. This is an iterative cycle based on giving more training data to the model. Product managers and business managers need to think about what function the AI can offer, how it can solve their business problem, and what data can they offer to help train the algorithm to create the right model. It is important to understand that more training data does not just mean more volume of training data always. It might mean that the training data used does not cover all possible scenarios and needs new training data that fills the gaps. For example, a computer vision model looking at lettuce sprouts to pick the best ones to grow to get a better crop yield might have a 60% confidence. The business person might be able to look at the training data and find out that the model fails to spot crops at a certain time of the day when the sun casts a shade on the field. So getting training data of images of the lettuce field in the shade might contribute to training the model better. So a business or product manager understanding how the algorithm works and what metrics it tracks will help them get the right training data for the AI researcher to iterate the AI algorithm toward better business results.

Figure: Autonomous Vehicle (AV) built as a test system of system by Phil Magney of VSI labs to demonstrate the integration of multiple IoT sensors in the AV. The two screens show the output of thermal sensors and object recognition from cameras.   Picture by Sudha Jamthe at ArmTechCon 2019 conference Automotive Pavilion.

Chapter 6: AIX Case Studies: AI Modeling for Business Success

6.1 AI Hierarchy of Needs

In this chapter we bring you case studies from a variety of businesses from around the world, covering multiple industries, teaching us the best practices, the reality of how to apply AIX, and how to use data to design AI models that have a positive business impact.

The bulk of the work in successful AI models for business success focuses on organizing, cleaning and structuring the data with business acumen or domain knowledge.

Monica Rogati has developed an AI hierarchy of Need to guide the data preparation needed for AI modelling, as shown in the future below. It begins with collecting the data correctly and instrumenting the right metrics to collect. Is the data collected every 5 minutes or every 30 minutes. It is combined with external data feeds? Next is the infrastructure to move the data. If data is collected at the edge inside a car, what is the infrastructure by which it is moved and stores. Is it structured or unstructured data? Next comes cleaning the data and preparing the data for what it is meant to be used for. Next comes an important step of labeling the data. This is when numbers and pictures come to life with meaning. Then comes the algorithms and A/B testing. Finally comes the building of the AI.

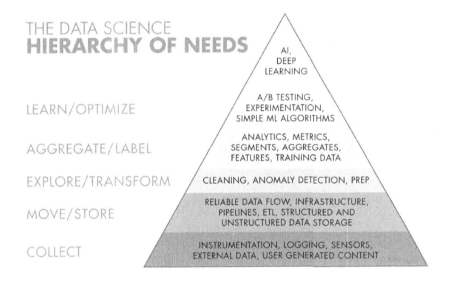

Figure: Monica Rogati's AI hierarchy of Need   Credit: Monica Rogati

6.2 Key to Successful AI Modeling in Companies

Partnership between IT and Business in Defining Training Data

Typically the AI Modelling job is split between the business or product manager and a technologist. Feature Engineering is in the process of using business acumen or domain knowledge to extract features that can be used to organize the data that trains the algorithms to improve their performance. This is done in partnership between the ML developer or Information Technology team and business team as an iterative exercise.

1. The "Business Data Scientist" who will do feature engineering, data preprocessing and initial models e.g. in KNMIE or Rapidminer or Python. And see if a business case can be made.

2. The "machine learning engineers" optimizes a Proof of Concept (PoC) and pushes it to production.

You can see this demonstrated in the case studies from industry practitioners below. Farlang case study is a classic example of how they build a Personalization AI as an iteration over many years in partnership between technology and business teams, where they used each iteration to create a deeper understanding of their customer.

Building an inexpensive MVP (Minimum Viable Product) or Pilot or Proof of Concept (PoC)

One option is to build a pilot as a proof of concept and define a minimum viable product. This could be done inexpensively with sensors and boards readily available in the market. Once you test and see results, you can do user research with this pilot and then decide to scale. This is especially helpful in large companies because having a proof of concept with results to show the business value will help convert some business units that initially resisted the change. This is one of the reasons many companies have innovation centers, where they test innovation ideas and build out AI models to test with some early adopter customers, and then bring it to the larger company subsequently.

One caveat with this method is that you have to be aware that you cannot scale a model past a certain point to show business results unless you work with the real business unit with real customer data.

This is where many IoT and AI pilots get stuck, in what is known as 'POC hell' where they build a proof of concept and then seem to be iterating endlessly and not scaling to production.

I have seen businesses go through this, and heard from technology people who are frustrated that they are not getting the right data to scale the model, and from business who distrust their technology teams and think that they need to apply a different algorithm to create better results. Most of the time, it is a disconnect between them. In many large enterprises, there is the IT vs OT divide. IT has limited access to customer data, but has the technological skills to build technology solutions. OT, or the operating business units, have customer data that they protect and the domain knowledge about what the data means. This has happened over the years in many industries for a variety of technological adoptions. It is even more prevalent with AI solutions than in the past.

In AI models, there is an iteration needed to build the algorithm using training data. Then the algorithm has to be modeled for business use cases. If this is done as two discrete steps, there will naturally be a disconnect. This is especially true with anomaly detection, where it is inherently difficult to know what metrics need to be tracked. It is complicated by the fact that the definition of normal is so tied to the business use case and the models are often created by technologists in isolation. Also, the business person who is unaware of the differences between the various algorithms and the different situations they can be used for can be unreasonably demanding of the technologists. I hope these case studies demystify the reality of the challenges and the best practices that have been employed by teams that have overcome this challenge. Also, in the Appendix, find a list of commonly used algorithms and their business uses. I have also added an Appendix of common problems data scientists get stuck on and seek answers during the AI modeling process.

Transient State of AI Modeling Tools Today:

In any exponential technology in early stages there are many startups offering foundational technologies. These startups shutdown or get acquired as the market matures. With AI, the speed with which the technologies are surfacing and dying is high. These startups emanate from open source communities and then become pivotal before getting acquired but they become proprietary once acquired by large technology companies.

One such example is KubeFlow. It was promoted by Google engineering and the community became very strong before the very active member, Chris Fregly and his company PipelineflowAI that works on top of TensorFlow got acquired by AWS. Clients from companies deployed on competing cloud platforms might distrust the product now that it is owned and hosted on a competing cloud solution.. Companies end up ripping out the stack repeatedly and rebuilding from scratch when startups are acquired by competition. Vinay Manglani, CEO of VigourSoft who has a team of Machine Learning engineers build AI models for clients, shared his experience on the impact shifting AI tools have on his enterprise clients building AI models. "Once a client refused to use AWS because Amazon was their competitor and we were using some native services including tons of Lambda functions. Another time we had to move from Scala to Java spring boot for the data access layer from a lack of resources. There is a lack of standardization in AI and unified approach unlike what we saw in the days of Java. While technical challenges are fun for engineers and profitable for engineering services vendors, it does add cost burden and has a serious impact on the time-to-market for the solution providers."

Particularly in the AI space, the problem of startups being acquired by larger technology companies is common, because AI tech talent is scarce. Many startups build foundational AI modeling tools or algorithms that meet specific industry client's needs, only to get

acquired as talent acquisitions lead to lost time and rework for
enterprise clients

6.3 Managing the Shift in AI Modeling Tools

As we discussed at the start of the book, there are two AI Business
markets. One of the technology companies racing to build AI models
that can be used out of the box by industry clients. The other is
enterprise companies going through a digital transformation
journey by looking into their data assets and applying algorithms
and combining with open datasets to do AI modelling to arrive at AI
models with satisfactory performance that they can use to solve
business problems of operational efficiency or strategic business
growth. So it is important to be aware what kind of AI business are
you building where you are using AI modeling tools and are affected
by their shifts as startups change focus or get acquired. One
common area I see this in Autonomous Vehicle space is with
perception technology. There are many startups focusing on
perception AI to offer a map on how the car can see the road using
object recognition and neural network algorithms. So when a
company such as Voyage.auto decides to build upon a startup
offering a perception AI, they have to be aware of what happens if

this startup is bought by a competitor, maybe a large car maker who is also making Robotaxis.

Build versus Buy Decision

If you are an enterprise with data looking to apply AI to transform your business, it is important to add this to your consideration on how much you are building your solution to be reliable on any startup that could exit by being bought by competition. This is a typical buy versus build decision IT is used to making. You need to make it now at the AI modeling stage.

Make a Strategic Investment in the AI Tool Startup

If you are a large company, you could invest financially in the startup that is going to be a strategic foundation to your AI solution and thereby hedge your bets. Or you could build redundancy into your solution by using two vendors in parallel so you have a fail-over option. The final option is to seek out open datasets and open source software and AI models to use in your work and to fort out a branch and start building on it for your industry.

Today AI Modelling is challenging for many companies. But if the AI you build is a critical part of your digital transformation, it is smart to invest your company resources to contribute to open source to create open standards for your industry.

6.4: List of AIX case studies

1. Case Study: Blockchain for Energy Consumption

2. Case Study: Chatbot for Carrier's Customer Support

3. Case Study: AI based Quality Control of Oil Refinery

4. Case Study: Digital Transformation of Smart Building

5. Case study: McDonald's Personalized Menu at Drive-thru

6. Case Study: AI in Healthcare - Listening Out for Us

7. Case Study: Omnichannel Personalization for Retail

8. Case Study: Low Cost Computer Vision with Arm

9. Case Study: Automated Building Management

10. Case Study: Retail Ad platform

1. Case Study: Blockchain for Energy Consumption

Thanks to Alex D'Elia aka acme of Mangrovia Blockchain Solutions.

SUDHA JAMTHE

Company Background:

Mangrovia Blockchain Solutions is two year old, a top ten "Blockchain Development" company (as recognized by Gartner in 2019) based in Milan, Italy. Mangrovia offers software solutions to foster the decentralized governance and infrastructure model for energy companies based on Blockchain Decentralized Ledger Technology (DLT). PROSUME is the subsidy of Mangrovia that supports energy distributors.

Business Problem:

PROSUME energy subsidy helps energy stakeholders to simplify and automate the process of balancing, exchange and integration of settlement procedures for accounting and contracting purposes. Meter and submeter devices have constant flow of meter measures and the data is manageable. When data comes aggregated from multiple databases there is no standard format, sometimes it is scrambled. Sometimes it is not precise. Some data comes in Excel files exceeding the 500,000 lines. The scale and complexity makes it time consuming to sift through this data manually. Biggest challenges are corruption, reluctant action by too old players, monopolized market and regulatory framework.

AIX

Product/Solution:

Mangrovia, when analyzing the data sets coming from different sources Mongrovia PROSUME, decided to use Machine Learning to process the data to organize the data to look for efficiencies. They developed a metering, recording, stamping and monitoring of metered data module, automated payments, an aggregator module, Integrated into IoT and fiscal meter devices and created a trading platform at the Transmission System Operator (TSO) level. TSO is a term defined by the European Commission. A TSO is an entity responsible for transporting energy in the form of natural gas or electrical power on a national or regional level, using fixed infrastructure.

Challenge Solved with Data:

Mangrovia mostly stored data on meter devices and IoT. The real data ranged from 1 sec to 900 sec. Mangrovia standardized the data structure and found an efficient protocol to communicate it. They built a standard procedure to allow traders to reach the level of "Smart Contracting". They built a modular solution with various Blockchains, DLTs. They created the capability to plug-in new identity and privacy modules into the system to make it interoperable.

Key Takeaway

Simple Machine Learning was the AI used by Mangrovia to organize their data. Mongrovia was able to successfully standardize all data into the same structure. Only then could they run machine learning successfully to achieve business results.

References:

https://www.pv-magazine.com/2019/05/16/abb-evolvere-jointly-launch-blockchain-energy-pilot/

https://www.snam.it/en/Media/news_events/2020/Snam_first_transactions_with_blockchain_gas_market.html

2. Case Study: Chatbot for Carrier's Customer Support

Thanks to Ken Herron, CMO of UIB Holdings Pte. Ltd.

Company Background

Emirates Integrated Telecommunications Company, also known as du, is a telecom operator in the United Arab Emirates. It serves approximately 9 million customers with its mobile, fixed line and broadband services. du was named the "Best Mobile Broadband Network in the Middle East and Africa" region in 2012 by ARC Chart. du's annual revenue now exceeds AED 10 billion (US$2.7M).

Business Problem

With a goal of connecting with people more easily and to keep pace with evolving customer needs, du realized that it needed to provide people with a superior digital experience. It wanted to reach its customers via a familiar channel to help them with their queries.

Product/Solution

du's solution was to create a virtual assistant. du wanted to differentiate itself from the competition by using technology to effectively resolve customer queries and complaints. Because WhatsApp was already being used by a large proportion of UAE residents, du decided to work with it. The telco provider teamed up with communications and artificial intelligence expert UIB, which created Blu, a WhatsApp-powered virtual assistant. Through this virtual assistant, customers would be able to contact the business at all times. Following internal trials with employees, Blu was made available to the public through du's website in March 2019. Customers began reaching out via WhatsApp, initiating conversations with Blu about bill payments, roaming service activations, online order tracking, mobile recharge, and account registration.

Success Metrics

Since its launch in March 2019, thousands of people have interacted with du's WhatsApp-powered virtual assistant. Blu can reply to customers within a matter of seconds and has successfully reduced the volume of queries handled by du's call centers and stores. Other results include:

- 80% of customers chose to resolve their queries via WhatsApp
- More than 50% of customer inquiries were resolved via WhatsApp bot
- 50,000 customer conversations took place via the WhatsApp chatbot between March–September 2019

Key Takeaway

du wanted to reach its customers via a familiar channel to help them with their queries. The AI-powered virtual assistant was successfully built and deployed as a collaborative effort together with du's partner, and official WhatsApp Business Solution Provider, UIB. UIB built the virtual assistant using its UnificationEngine technology. This contributed to the focused innovation and launch, building upon the business knowledge of several departments. The project was scoped well with a focus on interoperability and respect for the privacy of customers.

References

https://www.facebook.com/business/success/du

https://www.du.ae/personal/support

https://uib.ai/a-first-for-du-and-their-customers/

3. Case Study: AI based Quality Control of Oil Refinery

Thanks to: Aleksander Poniewierski, Partner & Global IoT leader and Head of Digital and Emerging Technologies EMEIA, EY

The Company:

A large European oil refinery

Business Problem:

The refinery had a challenge related to quality control. Effective process control was hindered by the inability to directly observe or estimate a number of industrial process parameters. Product laboratory tests are expensive, lengthy, infrequently performed, and thus only allow a small number of samples to be tested. The process required a lab test every few hours. If the results of the lab tests were OK, then everything was fine. But if an issue was identified then the entire batch produced over these hours needed to be reprocessed. The quality of the product depended on multiple factors: temperature, humidity, etc. The relationship of these factors and final quality tests are too complex to comprehend.

Product:

Artificial intelligence was used to "reverse engineer" the model and the dependency between the factors and the final quality. Data Used: 2500 IoT sensor readings every minute analyzing in total 3 billion IoT data points. We used statistical models based on existing data as the basis of our approach. Historical process data from Operating and production data on process variables form OT systems (DCS, SCADA) was combined with laboratory test results for available measurements of the variable of interest – covering the same period as the operating and production data from the process.

Solution:

A new Intelligent Process Optimization (IPO) model to predict heat of combustion for diesel fuel was developed. The Solution was built on the real-time IoT data coming from the production environment, processed and enhanced with highly accurate data modeling that incorporated artificial neural networks and machine learning, and provides a real-time highly-accurate end-products' quality parameters forecasts. The Predictive Quality Concept is an advanced quality management model which delivers real-time visibility of product quality during the production process. The concept is based on modeling of the production process with Advanced Analytics techniques which discover correlations within the ecosystem of production process parameters. Predictive quality enables the possibility of timely alignment of production in order to secure required quality of end product. IPO leverages existing/new IoT soft sensors to develop and update models that predict the quality of a production process.

SUDHA JAMTHE

AI Algorithm used:

The client wanted to use a small number of inputs. The client wanted to run models on premise, but it had limited computational powers. Moreover, models with smaller numbers of inputs tend to give less noisy output. So a Machine Learning model with neural networks was used. We did data mining and advanced data transformations. *Stepwise forward selection*, a type of regression technique, was chosen because it works well with a small number of input variables. We began with an empty model with no inputs. Then we added one variable that gave the single best improvement to the model in each forward step and iterated to desired performance.

Success metric:

The results of prediction accuracy exceeded 90%, which was a 15% improvement over the model used earlier by the client. Based on the achieved results, the Client extended the program and engaged the Intelligent Process Optimization solution to improve another vital step in the refining process relying on multi parameter controls – fuel and additive blending.

> **Key Takeaway**
>
> Test and Iterate is a good way to improve the performance of AI models. Also building an AI model on one focused use case for a client is a good way to begin to help the company adapt AI solutions and build trust to use AI for business problems. This can then be expanded to solve other business problems for the same company.

4. Case Study: Digital Transformation of Smart Building

Credit: Dalton Oliveira, "IoT, IIoT, AI, and Global Information Systems (GIS) for Facilities Management".

Company:

A group that manages 5 Fab Lab's in the city of Sao Paulo, Brazil covering the entire city geographic area.

Business Problem:

The company wanted centralized management of the five Fab Labs to manage usage of the equipment in each Fab Lab energy efficiently.

Data Used:

Usage of the industrial equipment in each Fab Lab (Smart Industry, Industry 4.0) was collected by installing sensors in each piece of equipment, to gather audience numbers from each room with motion sensors at entrances and exits. All data in the local and remote network are in real-time. Building the dashboard with past infos (range of date) is based on stored data. Real-time data was gathered from sensors when triggered by a specific action - in this case, start/stop of the machines, entrance/exit of a user in the room, env conditions (temp, hum), etc. All data is stored in the cloud, which fuels the suite (chatbot, dashboards, legacy). A time series of sensor data per machine was collected every 30sec for 1 month, to file size about 5MB.

Solution:

A Digital Product #SmartyEnergy from Wardson.com, a suite of platforms that uses IoT and AI/chatbot for single user and dashboard for Leader Team - all data in cloud. The dashboard contains a map with a layer with bar graphs (quantified data) per region. It could use voice commands, but Fab Labs chose AI/chatbot as the interface for users.

Once we had the data that met the business need, more use cases and other easy-to-gather data were added, to build and "complete" the puzzle that would transform the entire business. In addition to industry equipment information, the sensors provide information about buildings. This was used to optimize process flow for the facilities dept.

Key Takeaway

This was not about IoT, AI/chatbot, and cloud only, this is about Digital Transformation (engineering, process, project, product, customer experience). Inside IT, many divisions: PM, developers, architects, DBA, network, infra, business departments and business teams and legal were involved directly, divided by Squads. The business provides information to build the data structure, the decision tree, the KB, what connects to which content, etc. that helps in choosing the right AI models to make the project a success.

---

5. Case study: McDonald's Personalized Menu at Drive-thru

Credit: David Kerrigan, Author, Life as a Passenger

Company:

With over 38,000 restaurants worldwide and annual sales of over $100 billion, McDonald's Corp. is a global fast food giant. Since 2017 it has embarked on a radical modernization plan, using new technology to remain relevant in a changing world.

Business Problem:

Faced with decreasing footfall to US stores, growing competition, difficulties recruiting staff and changing consumer tastes, McDonald's was urgently looking to boost revenues. Due to the complex supply chain and concerns about menu changes making serving times slower, McDonald's was especially interested in solutions that make more of the existing menu, while working on longer-term plans to improve the menu. When operating at the scale of McDonald's, the complexity of rollout can impact the viability of an otherwise beneficial initiative.

With about 65% of McDonald's revenue in the US coming from drive-thru sales, it's an obvious place for management to focus on driving efficiency. But the most recent survey shows McDonald's hasn't been doing well. According to QSR Magazine - at an average of 273 seconds per customer (vs. an industry average of 234 seconds), it lags far behind its major rivals. The QSR survey also showed that up to 58% of McDonald's drive thru customers weren't offered "suggested sells" - where the server encourages the customer to make additional purchases. A key factor in profitability, the uneven nature of human upsell, is a common challenge in many retail environments.

The Solution:

McDonald's identified personalization as a solution to present customers with more relevant offers. Serving some 68 million customers per day, McDonald's doesn't lack sales data but as former CEO Steve Easterbrook put it, "It's about drawing the insight and intelligence out of it." After evaluating multiple vendors, McDonald's implemented a trial with Israeli firm, Dynamic Yield.

Although a global franchise like McDonald's is built on consistency, there's always been a need for localization - dishes adopted to local preferences as well as the global favorites. But even within a country, there's a need for local factors to be considered and that's been impossible until now. With Dynamic Yield's technology, each customer at each McDonald's location can be shown a different menu, subtly altered to the time, place and specific restaurant situation.

Data used:

Obvious data inputs for menu personalization include the weather and the time of day. They can decide to offer customers more ice cream if the weather is warm and make hot drinks more prominent when it's cold. Static menus give equal prominence regardless of these readily available inputs. Less obvious factors that feed into the Dynamic Yield recommendation engine include real time stock availability in each restaurant - so no more menus that include items that aren't available. The new menu technology can also temporarily remove more complex items from the menu screens at busy times, to encourage customers not to order products that take longer to prepare as a means to protect those all-important time to serve metrics.

From a data point of view, even with over 60 million transactions per day, a fast food menu is a relatively small set of variables compared to a large retailers range. But tied with data about local conditions, restaurant stock and even previous customer orders, AI can tie the data together to be greater than the sum of its parts. But AI offers even more potential benefits for McDonald's beyond the customer facing improvements. The new technology will enable them to test new menus or promotions with efficiency comparable to an online business. Additional benefits will evolve as they apply this technology to inform inventory management, to improve sustainability and to even reduce waste.

In some jurisdiction, where it's legal and where customers have opted in, McDonald's is also trialing the use of license plate recognition to add another layer of data for the Dynamic Yield algorithms to consider - previous order history. A staple input for web based implementations of the technology, using licence plates as a way of recognizing repeat customers will enable McDonald's to offer truly personalized menus and very targeted upsell or loyalty offers.

Proprietary Technology

Dynamic Yield has developed a suite of algorithms and models to combine personalization & predictive targeting, recommendations, testing & optimization and behavioural messaging for clients such as Ocado, Urban Outfitters and Ikea. Its patent-pending technology powers experiences for 600 million users each month across hundreds of global brands. Its decisioning engine uses machine learning and predictive algorithms to build customer segments in real time that are then constantly refined, based on commercial performance.

Success metrics:

Beyond the important short term gains in drive thrus, McDonald's acquired Dynamic Yield for $300 Million USD. *"We're already seeing an increase in average check by improving our ability to offer customers what they are likely to want with suggestions based on time of day, weather, and items already in a customer's order"* - Steve Easterbrook, former CEO, McDonald's Dynamic Yield.

Like a lot of AI, it's quick to scale physically - McDonald's has deployed the technology to over 10,000 locations nationwide, with the time-consuming and expensive element of the rollout being the actual digital signs rather than the AI powering them. And compared to the $6bn recently invested in renovating stores, the AI investment could be self-sustaining with even a tiny uptick in average order value.

While the deployment of AI may seem very beneficial from a business point of view, as always, it's important to stop to consider the customer impact. Although customers appreciate shorter lines, and may not object to personalized recommendations that are relevant (and tasty!), there has been pushback reported across the fast food sector as some consumers find dynamic menus confusing.

Key Takeaway

This will help McDonald's with the digital transformation of their business, as they weave the technology into the wider business. The same recommendation technology can be adapted for use on in-store ordering kiosks (17,000+ globally) and adapted again for the mobile app that's increasingly popular for ordering deliveries in partnership with Uber Eats.

As an example of AI, McDonald's use of the technology embodies multiple trends - personalization, tech moving into physical retail and raises questions about privacy and customer experience. It's also an example of AI moving into everyday use with or without consumer awareness.

Conclusion:

McDonald's investment in AI appears to be paying off; others in the industry will follow. Sonic Drive-In has already announced it's testing similar personalized menus, while Taco Bell is adding AI to its mobile app to show users the most relevant menu items, promotions and content based on their individual preferences, past dining history, location, weather and restaurant specific menus and pricing.

6. Case Study: AI in Healthcare - Listening Out for Us

Credit: David Kerrigan, Author,The New Acceleration: An Introduction to Artificial Intelligence

Background

A team at the University of Washington has investigated the use of smartphones and smart speakers to listen for signs of cardiac arrest and then trigger an alert for help. Besides smartphones, only one other technology in history has been adopted by a ¼ of Americans in just 2 years - AI-powered voice assistants in smart speakers. Smart speaker sales have reached around 100 million - which means there's an unprecedented number of connected microphones across the nation.

Business Problem

Every year, hundreds of thousands of people die from cardiac arrest where no help is available, most commonly at home. With timely CPR, the chances of survival would be significant but in many cases, the victim is alone. In approximately half of the cases when someone experiences cardiac arrest, there is typically a very distinctive sound, known as "agonal breathing" as they struggle to breathe.

Solution & Technology

The UW team trained a model to listen, via smartphones or smart speakers, for agonal breathing, and then trigger an alert for help. The training data was obtained from 9-1-1 calls where the agonal breathing sound was audible and captured.

Using real-world labeled 9-1-1 audio of cardiac arrests, a *support vector machine (SVM) algorithm* was used to classify agonal breathing instances in real-time within a bedroom environment. In order to increase accuracy and reduce false positives, a negative dataset of ambient household noise and audio from polysomnographic sleep studies, which include data that share similar audio characteristics to agonal breathing such as snoring and obstructive apnea events, was also used in the training. The 9-1-1 emergency calls, provided by Public Health-Seattle & King County, Division of Emergency Medical Services included 162 calls that had clear recordings of agonal breathing. Given the relatively small size of the agonal breathing dataset, the number of agonal breathing instances was augmented with *label preserving transformation*, a common technique applied to sparse datasets.

Acoustic interference cancellation was also used to reduce the interfering effects of the speakers/smartphones and improve detection accuracy of agonal breathing - when the audio cancellation algorithm is applied, the detection accuracy achieves an average accuracy of 98.62 and 98.57% across distances and sounds for soft and loud interfering volumes, respectively.

Key Takeaway

AI technology can be implemented with out-of-box models on a low budget. Iterating models and data structures at the same time required alignment of many different stakeholders, to better hone in on emotions and cognition behind a traditional sales process. Relevant data was critical, far more than "big data". You do not have to wait for a use dataset to train a model to save lives. You can use creative methods to increase scarce dataset and to remove false positives to get good quality training data.

Conclusions & Next Steps

Non-contact, passive detection of agonal breathing represents a novel way to identify a portion of previously unreachable victims of cardiac arrest. As the US population ages and more people become at risk for OHCA, leveraging commodity smart hardware for monitoring of these emergent conditions could have public health benefits.

An immediate concern of a passive agonal breathing detector is privacy. For this use case, intentional activation of the device (i.e., "Hey Alexa" or "Hey Siri") immediately prior to classification is not feasible because diagnosis involves an unconscious individual in an emergent situation. To address privacy concerns, they authorize the system to run locally on the smart devices and not store any data.

Although a small study, the results are promising and the authors suggest several methods for continued analysis.

Reference:

https://www.nature.com/articles/s41746-019-0128-7 includes the code created (on github) and contact details for the authors who may provide access to the training data if deemed reasonable.

7. Case Study: Omnichannel Personalization for Retail

Credit: C.Friederich, Mah Rana, Patrick Slavenburg

Company Background:

Farlang, launched in 2005, became the world's 2nd largest platform focused on luxury jewelry, diamonds, and gemstones. Placing this into perspective, the American jewelry market in 2015 was estimated to be around $70 billion, the luxury segment roughly $10 billion. Farlang was revolutionary in two ways. They focused on self-purchasing women long before others and they expanded the designer's customer base by targeting new and light buyers. Light buyers are those who only purchase once or a few times over a lifetime. In contrast, designers traditionally had focused on building life-long relationships with repeat-buyers and retail partners. The difference is important because of the need to offer relevant products at the correct time with little room for error.

The second was a serious resistance to disruptive change in an industry which relied upon traditions that were "tried & proven" amongst male consumers, but no longer effective with a new and more modern female clientele.

In order to accomplish our objective of having the right product at the precise moment, a Lean UX approach was adopted with continuous iteration over customer experiences.

Problem Definition

How to create personalization algorithms for online, in-store, and private event use. Ninety percent (90%) of designs were one-of-a-kind. As a consequence, any recommendation algorithm would operate deep into the "long tail", our tail being particularly "fat", i.e. the entire product could be considered part of the long tail. Product catalog was not diverse given the new audience. Any type of behavioral algorithm correlating divergent products based on behavioral data alone has a high propensity to be spurious, and not a good predictor of the next visitor's taste or interest.

Unique AI/Data Challenges:

It was a challenge to understand what drove business value and what did not. Not coincidentally, jewelry retail (online & offline) had traditionally resorted to "safe bets" by showing "more of the same designer," more of the same color (gemstone), more of the same metal, or other factors which tend to be void of emotion or personal preference. Many designs were so unique they could trigger visitor behavior for a variety of reasons. Only a few of those behaviors correlated to "buyer interest". That's a small signal in a vast ocean of noise. Basing a recommendation algorithm on visitor behavior alone - without understanding their underlying cognitive processes and emotions - just amounts to spurious correlations that do not produce a sale ("correlating a whole bunch of noise").

AI modelling approach

An entirely new conceptual framework for personalization had to be invented. Traditionally, all jewelry sales are focused on the product and the artist. Cost, rarity of materials, skillset or craftsmanship were characteristics of how gift-giving men decided upon purchases. Women, however, focused on stylised factors such as skin tone, personality expression, and how it pulled together a specific fashion "look". Different *style tribes* were developed paying close attention to social settings, status, and context as well as symbolism and more abstract concepts which captured a specific sentiment for an occasion, a lifestyle, or a personality preference. For example Madeleine Allbright was famous for wearing brooches sending a "hidden message" about her position to those with whom she was negotiating.

Data Used

The project was rolled out in different stages over several years as we needed more and better data to underpin improving user experiences, behaviour, and personalisation nuances.

Version 1. Understanding the product and consumer.

1. **Labeling data for images, a visual vocabulary/ontology:** As computer vision could not deliver image features since it was not sophisticated enough, different jewelry by different designers were photographed under different angles. To extract stylistic, emotional, and design features under those conditions would have been impossible. Therefore we manually labeled them using text.

2. **Visitor behavior data on website:** Relying on Google analytics alone was insufficient. So we also used other analytics plugins, heatmap tracking, and many years worth of website data collected.

Version 2. Understanding the context and emotion.

3. **Key insights data from experts**: We capitalised on those who made understanding the mindset and emotional drivers of women, fashion, and style through the use of the domain knowledge of stakeholders: designers, gem experts, retailers, fashion leaders, influencers, personal stylists, psychologists, authors - and codifying this data e.g. in "rules" engines.

   Version 3+. Demographics, finding the right client and the best place for a product.

4. **US Census Open data:** US Census data entirely cleaned database confidentially shared by Gilt Groupe was used through an API from the US Census site.
5. **Geolocation data:** "Digitalelement" software physically verified IP addresses.
6. **Retailer customer data:** Historic data about customer usage from retailer's database was used.

Solution

The solution was not about the complexity of the model or perfecting a model as much as about combining different models and using the "right" heuristics from experts as well as technology.

AIX

In other words, Farlang did not rely on "machine learning" alone to do the heavy lifting. Instead they augment emotions and behavior when it made sense and codified them into heuristics.

Time and resources were not wasted training computers to do what is best left to humans.

Although fashion changes regularly, the sentiments and personalities behind individual purchases tend to be less volatile, i.e. a woman's past experiences, environment, etc. are better indicators, which do not change nearly as quickly nor have deep underlying emotional patterns.

The above mentioned insights and approaches allowed us to pre-process recommendations as much as possible in batch processing 1x per night. This left a relatively small part to processing in real time - and thus created much less severe engineering challenges (and thus lowered deployment costs).

Version 1

Item Based Recommendation: Analyzing the description of Content Only. How can you find similarities between items? Assumption is at least a weak correlation between "design" and "taste".

- A team tagged each item with an ontology using Art Theory "Design Elements & Principles". In later versions we labelled images with an additional "emotional and style" ontologies.

- A "bag of words" approach was applied to the labels of each item creating a vector. For classification/clustering, we used the least complex unsupervised models s.a. K-means (e.g. calculating Euclidean distance or Pearson's Correlation).

- This approach helped with the Cold Start Problem.

- The result was a dramatic (200-400%) increase in click through rates compared to traditional methods such as "more of this designer" resulting in loss of a sale opportunity. However, in terms of sales enquiries (one of the conversion metrics we used) we only saw a small uptick (10% or so).

Version 2

Our visual vocabulary was changed and expanded to focus on "tribes". The "Tribe" was the feature we wanted to predict rather than specific jewelry items. The uncertainty around an individual item prediction was simply too large to be useful. Using the concept of "tribes" however made an enormous difference. Time saved and frustration avoidance of pin-pointing the appropriate product for a client was useful to all those involved. It was especially important to the client who had little time to devote to shopping.

Again like in Version 1, both classification and (basic) rules engines were implemented to help with color and physical style attributes, tribes, lifestyle, occasions, and other personalization criteria. This resulted in a dramatic improvement in sales enquiries by 100-200% after several iterations.

Version 3

Building a user profile, geodemographics, and expanding to in-store events, helped our jewelry and gemstone designers and - in the case of in-store events - retailers find the right clients and save time by presenting them with the most relevant products.

Expanding data sets with "IP geolocation at street level" + US Census data + proprietary research on "style tribes", we could match a "visitor vector" to a "product cluster vector" and improve the relevance of our recommendations with another 50% or so. As with previous versions we preferred to keep things simple using the most common - both supervised and unsupervised - classification algorithms.

For in-store events, it allowed us to "profile" invited customers (of whom we had customer data s.a. address) in ways a retailer had never been able to, not even for their repeat customers. We could also make a "probabilistic profile" of walk-in traffic during an event.

For all these new and light customers, this approach is the equivalent of solving the "cold start problem" online. Based on those analyses, we could match which designers from our community would be the best match for sales or custom design work at the event.

Key Takeaway

AI technology can be implemented with out-of-box models on a low budget. Iterating models and data structures at the same time required alignment of many different stakeholders, to better hone in on emotions and cognition behind a traditional sales process. Relevant data was critical, far more than "big data".

8. Case Study: Low Cost Computer Vision with Arm

Thanks: Jeff Fryer, Arm

Company: A Silicon Valley data company named Silicon Valley Data Science.

Project: The company wanted to detect Caltrain delays, to differentiate among five types of trains. They had no reliable dataset to use for predictions, but had access to watch a real Caltrain, which they monitored with cameras to capture videos to use as training data for a Computer Vision model.

Technology: Raspberry Pi meets AI, thanks to Arm

Solution:

They set up a system to monitor the trains running on a specific route and detect Caltrain among a host of other trains like freight, light rails etc., and then classified the types of trains captured on video.

To detect Caltrain in this system, a classification of different trains was needed, which was achieved by deploying TensorFlow on Arm to create this system using a Raspberry Pi 3. The system cost $130 to build and required little knowledge of TensorFlow to deploy. This decision was made in order to keep it affordable, and to avoid what would be massive delays in sending images to a central server without the benefit of high speed internet. It was possible to do TensorFlow image recognition on a Raspberry Pi in real time, run at the edge. DIY AI image recognition, all enabled by Arm.

Technology: Raspberry Pi 2B (feat Arm Cortex-A53) with accessories, Pi Camera, case for GoPro mount and GoPro wall mount, and a Wi-Fi adapter -- with total cost of $130. Using TensorFlow on Arm and JupyterHub for software and services.

Key Takeaway

AI technology can be implemented with out-of-box models on a low budget. Iterating models and data structures at the same time required alignment of many different stakeholders, to better

---

> hone in on emotions and cognition behind a traditional sales
>
> process. Relevant data was critical, far more than "big data".

References:

Link: https://svds.com/tensorflow-image-recognition-raspberry-pi

http://www.svds.com/streaming-video-analysis-python/ (focused on how to do streaming video analysis with python)

9. Case Study: Automated Building Management

Credit: Sai Allavarpu, VP & GM, Danaher Digital

Company:

Commercial buildings/facilities management enterprise business with multi-billion dollar revenues across all major geos in the world was originally an equipment provider: e.g. HVAC controllers, boilers, compressors and chillers (aka RTU - RoofTop Units) found typically on top of buildings, indoor thermostats and comfort controllers. The company wanted to increase its operational efficiencies and increase business growth with digital led services.

Business Problem:

The business had two business goals they wanted to achieve by using digital connectivity and data that motivated this transition to become a service business. They wanted to reduce labor and energy costs of managing energy and comfort in those facilities. They also wanted to prevent unplanned shutdowns, be proactive in maintenance schedules and improve utilization and yield of equipment.

Data Used

Enterprise data: All "OT" data from connected IoT equipment: operational/machine data + facilities/building data such as floor plans, vent locations, per-floor/zone occupancy, office/event schedules, contractor availability/calendar/pricing rates/etc, inventory, etc.

Open/3rd party datasets: Energy consumption segmented by utility districts; other building energy consumption data (anonymized), high resolution weather data, geo-specific holidays data, etc. Open Datasets used were public weather data sets and location datasets.

Data was not real time but near-real time with streaming datasets for OT and environmental data. For third-party datasets, it was mostly "batch" data. Data fabric architecture was designed to handle both types of datasets coming in.

AI Modelling Challenge:

Data cleansing and prep was the biggest chunk of the work to get the data "AI-Ready" (formatting, missing values or units, duplicates, cross-data associations, etc).

The AI Solution:

Multi-vector product/solution: SaaS and mobile apps for building occupants to control their comfort settings (AC/heat/occupancy/etc). Occupancy sensors. SaaS/mobile apps for facilities operators/maintenance as well as for service contractors (including work order creation, dispatch, scheduling, post-service reports, etc). Also, new dashboards and KPI reports for senior leadership and financial stakeholders of facilities (costs, energy and labor optimization, peer-benchmarking, etc).

AI Technology/Algorithms used:
ML and AR (for equipment repairs or facilities walk-thru for repair/service technicians).

Next Steps: Energy and labor (thereby financial) forecasting and reporting, predicting energy usage spikes, predicting equipment failure or underperformance (increased energy use), recommendations on comfort (heat/cool) settings based on weather, utility rates, etc., anomaly detection in equipment operations, predicting and managing building occupancy, etc

Success Metrics:

Early on, metrics were #equipment units covered, #blds covered and #occupants served. Upon scaling, it changed to #customer conversions to paid subscription contracts, service contracts and pull-thru of equipment sales and competitive displacements.

10.Case Study: Retail Ad platform

Thanks to Vinaj Manglani, CEO VigourSoft

Company Background: A large scale media experimentation startup working in the retail domain. The softwaresolution is helping ecommerce brands optimize digital media spends and performance. They wanted to improve customer conversion using data and AI.

This is a use case of how ads and marketing dollars can be predictively utilized to derive more customer conversions for the same budget each time.

Business Solution:

VigourSoft partnered with the retail Ad company with AI and data engineering skills. They developed intelligent predictive experimentation algorithms that decipher the best and highest revenue generating combinations of products, ad platforms, ad groups, campaign parameters, audiences, campaign times and other such variable parameters. ROI is being able to predict and effectively channelize each ad and marketing dollar for better customer conversions.

Data Used:

A synthetic data generator written in Python was used to get the required data set for testing purposes. It was intended to test the solution with data at a scale of terabytes from three years of historical data. However, due to the sensitivity of information and due to compliance requirements, this was not possible. The partner was provided with a close match data profile that we used to generate synthetic data using our VigourSoft's home grown synthetic data generator tool. Our dataset was clean, with and verifiable outcomes. Data generated had information regarding purchase history/behaviour, what specific purchase (items) and how much quantity, what was the value of the purchase etc. Data sources were email transactions/web transactions/over the counter transactions, etc.

The solution, which took a disparate form of large number of input data sources, created a data pipeline that would be helpful not only to provide insights but also in predictive models. Output of data pipeline was loaded into high performance analytics data store (AWS Redshift). This became a single point of solution from ETL to media platform. High end UI (using angular stack) was built, which became a visual 360 platform for brands to get insights on their customer.

Challenges:

a) Availability of the right set of data set at the right time.

b) Long cycles for data ingestion needed for key business decisions (in some cases it took us 3-4 weeks to onboard the customers due to the complexity of data available and also for handling the volume).

c) Manual classification of the Users' data, which comes from different sources.

d) Masking and transferring of sensitive data (programmatically). AWS-IAM was used to store the private keys that were used to authenticate requests for decrypting the PIIs (Personally identifiable information) when needed.

Once we had a dataset, the next challenge was to get more insight (Customer360) into the data and come up with the right kind of predictions. We used below techniques/ML algorithms: a) Clustering algorithms (K-Means) to classify/cluster for customer segmentation based on parameters like shopping behaviour/recent purchases/Frequency of purchases/Value of purchases etc., and b) within each segment, we also had to come up with predictions in terms of when and how much this customer will come back for future purchases. We used the last 6-8 months purchase history/items history to come up with their needs. This was the Prediction model.

Success metric:

For data pipeline building, success metrics were: a) How much time was reduced to ingest the dataset (improved lead time for data ingestion, b) UI Performance in terms of how quickly users can get the requested data, c) Right classification of the customer segmentation and feedback from customers regarding accuracy of the same.

SECTION II: DESIGN

<u>What you will learn in this section</u>

1. Learn the final piece of the puzzle in AIX, the UX design of Artificial Intelligence or AIxDesign. Learn how about User Experience Design using data. How do you design a human centered Human Computer Interface using data?

2. Get an in-depth lesson about what it takes for you as a product designer to design for Voice, be it voice assistants or voice to the car.. As a designer you have the power to humanize the AI. Learn designing for Machine Learning (MLUX).

3. Designing for AI involves a transition to work with data but it still needs the usual design process that you are so familiar with today. What is new and what are transferable skills you can bring to new AI design jobs?

Figure: Kiwibot autonomous foot delivery robot carries around food in Berkeley, California.

When one of the kiwibots burnt down, Berkeley students put candles around it as a vigil. It is an example of how a robot experience can get humanized and accepted by people. Designing an AI or robot that is driven by data powering its autonomous algorithm now is in the hands of designers. We will learn about designing the AI or device persona in the next section when we delve into designing for Voice and Machine Learning.

CHAPTER 7: AIxDesign by Dr. Charles Ikem

AI is dominating the emerging technology space and as much attention from the design community, that has been yearning to automate interactions, design systems, and processes. AIXDesign is the design of algorithms that determine the behavior of intelligent systems. So, how do we shape the machine experience? How do we translate data into user interfaces and prototypes that are intuitive and useful? And how do we apply human-centered design to AI applications from ideation to user research, wireframing, coding, prototyping and finally, interfaces that perfectly mirror the intended behavior of algorithms in a sensible and humane manner.

AIXDesign is about designing the system behavior (voice, UI, taptics, haptics) and the overall experience involving AI from a human-centered perspective.

Two Ways to approach designing with AI:

How we approach AI will determine how we need to design it.

AI as a product:

Traditionally, we design emotion and behavior through a product's tone of voice like colors or product category. Then we moved to designing interactions and experiences. Now we have to contend with designing certain user and product behavior powered by AI. Think of the journey and output of creating an AI-enabled voice interface for customers like Amazon ECHO. Another example is deploying a machine learning model to identify objects in an Autonomous Vehicle.

The process for creating such a model involves:

- A generic algorithm with a basic description of outcome- object type, color, category
- Addition of constraints
- Independent variables such as humans with objects, cars, scooters
- Training the model

Then you have to think of the following:

- Designing a UI to describe the flow of I/O (could be voice, visual or a combination)
- Communicating error/unknown input
- Product/system behavior

AI as a tool:

AI is already changing the way designers solve problems. By developing algorithms that help automate the design process such as design systems that help with creating consistent patterns and styles.

UI personalization: Think of the system that personalizes the UI of your tracklist and recommending songs according to your past preferences and searches. Each line of code should have a basic description for UI and a series of UI's that link a particular track or genre that the system will select at any given time. The designer will need to think through the series of events and possibilities to create a pattern of UI preferences that will make use of the available code. AI as a tool is about feeding the system with data and then directing it to act.

To summarize, AIXDesign is about designing system behavior, which can be applied in two different ways. One is to design AI as a product where you design system behavior and interactions for a product. The second is to design AI as a tool where you use AI to automate design systems and processes.

AIxDesign Framework by Dr. Charles Ikem:

As designers, the user should always be at the center of our design. When designing with AI, you start with the users' needs and understand user behavior patterns. Then, look at the data and figure out how AI will improve the user's experience. Then, decide what kind of interface will enable user behavior and how users will interact with the AI output. Finally, think about how we visualize the data as output or feedback for the user to experience it.

For example, let us look at a user who is very price conscious and looking for the best travel deal. The user behavior is to focus on price and finding the deal quickly. We could look at data from various airlines to have an algorithm find options for the user as a recommendation. Since the user is price-conscious, we could use machine learning on past price patterns to predict whether now is a good time to buy the ticket or recommend that the user wait and watch for a better price in the next few days.

Next, we can look at the interface where this makes sense. We do not need voice or computer vision or some visual interface except a web or mobile app to interact with the user. Visually we can show the price predictions as a graph for the user to see the recommendation, similar to what Kayak.com shows on its travel site. Finally, we should think about how we are presenting data visually for the user. In this case, the user does not need to see a huge data feed. They can just see the recommended list of flights and their price, and go through a shopping flow.

In another example, the user is driving in a car while looking for the same travel deal, but this customer is very sensitive to travel durations. Looking at the figure below, we can see how AI will help the user behavior, and decide that voice will help while they are busy driving. In this case, AI can take the form of voice in the car, similar to Alexa Auto and the machine learning feed of airline ticket options, to find the best price and shortest duration for the user. The final step is about presenting the data to the user. Voice technology can make this a very user-friendly experience by requesting that the user provide desired travel dates and destination while driving. The system can then provide the user with options, also verbally, and the user can confirm flight, or ask for

more information, all while continuing to drive safely.

In all, applying the principles of human-centered design allows you

to create products and tools that are useful, usable and human-like.

Figure:

01 USER NEEDS
Identify user needs and behavior patterns

02 DATA NEEDS
How will AI support user needs & behavior patterns?

03 INTERFACE TYPE
What type of interface will enable user behavior and how will users interact with AI output. How do we visualize data?

AIxDesign Framework by Dr. Charles Ikem

AIXDesign encourages collaboration between AI engineers and

designers, to create AI-enabled products and custom tools.

CHAPTER 8: Design Process of AIX

When we design a product for AI, what is the difference between designing that product for different kinds of AI? For example, when we design a voice assistant to engage with customers inside the car, is there a difference between how we design the experience compared to sensors in the same car creating an Augmented Reality experience for the same user? When I worked at eBay designing product experiences across multiple mobile platforms such as iPhone, iPad, Android and Mobile Web, a multi-screen experience centered on the customer. We used data to understand when the customer used a different mobile interface and whether they expected a different experience on different platforms. For example, when iPhone introduced fingerprinting, the user expected fingerprinting to login on iPhone and was comfortable to login by entering their login on the mobile web when they used Safari on the same iPhone.

When designing for AI, customers just want to do whatever they have set out to do with your product. So it is important as a product designer to understand if there is a difference in customer expectation when using different AI and what you can offer to enhance their overall experience. Typically these days, AI design is done for multiple interfaces such as voice, sensor tracking haptic feedback, touch and text. This is called **multimodal interaction design**.

In this chapter you will learn the design process of working with data to build multimodal design interface products that work with Voice and Machine Learning and what is unique about designing for each of these AI interfaces.

8.1 Designing for Voice (VUI)

Voice Assistants use three AI Algorithms. They listen to our voice using voice recognition. They then convert the speech to text using speech recognition and then try to understand what we are asking of them using Natural Language Processing (NLP). NLP uses the semantics of language as a pattern to make sense of text. Then they use text to speech, to facilitate human-like communication using voice as the interface. Voice recognition is recognition of the actual audio voice itself. Alexa and Google Home now offer users the choice to allow them to identify each person's voice in the family using the same device. Today we are in early stages with Voice as an interaction mode, though voice seems to be getting adoption as a preferred mode for machine interaction. Voice command is especially popular among sports fans who want to watch a specific team on television but do not know what channel the game is on. It is getting adoption with voice assistants that are moving from our home to the car, hospitals and customer support chatbots on the phone. Voice design is waiting for you, the designer to create the right AIX user-centered design experience.

When designing for Voice, both the machine and human do not know the context of where the other is during a voice conversation. For example, on a web site, the cursor is always at a specific point on the screen, so there is context to indicate what the human is selecting and where they can be guided next. In Voice, the user can lose context because of the lack of a visual interface. So the designer needs to add some voice script that repeats what the user can expect from the Voice Assistant.

SUDHA JAMTHE

Voice UI Design Framework

When designing for Voice, the application can be a standalone application, such as a voice assistant like s Alexa with Amazon Echo or Google Home Assistant.

See figure below, a post from Steve Bishop, head of UX for Alexa Auto. Alexa Auto is bringing Alexa Voice Assistant to Lamborghini cars to help the driver use voice while driving to find navigation information or set the temperature setting inside the car.

Steven Bishop • 1st
Head of UX, Alexa Auto
1w • ⊗

Alexa and Lamborghini -- See if for yourself at the Alexa Auto booth in the North hall at CES2020. #alexa #voicefirst #ces #cars #automotive #lamborghini

Is your Lamborghini too cold? Just ask Alexa to heat it up

AIX

Figure: Alexa Auto is in Lamborghini cars. image credit: Sudha Jamthe from Steve's LinkedIn post from CES 2020

Bosch put a voice assistant called 'Casey' in the car in 2018. "When drivers get into a modern car, they can sometimes feel like an airplane pilot – buttons, screens, a confusing menu navigation with a thousand sub-menus. Bosch is putting an end to the button chaos in the cockpit. Instead, we turn the voice assistant into a passenger," says Dr. Dirk Hoheisel, Member of the Board of Management of Robert Bosch GmbH.

Figure: Bosch voice in the car

Voice in the Car and Impact on Car Brands

A fascinating but easy to overlook aspect of this transformation to voice interaction relates to the difference between communicating with your auto by voice and using a home assistant like Alexa or Google Home. In your home, you speak to a physical speaker unit, which now includes alternative devices like Alexa mini or Google Nest Home with its visual screen. At home, we feel like we are talking to a device or a "thing." When the voice moves to the car, even with the same Alexa voice offering the same kind of voice interaction, something shifts in our relationship with the device. For one, we do not see Alexa as a physical speaker unit. Instead the voice comes from inside the car, so it feels like we are talking to the car. Now the car has a personality with the voice.

This massive shift in human-computer interaction significantly impacts existing brands. Established auto brands cannot underestimate the significance of giving their cars voice personas. The designer has much of the power to set the AI persona with the voice, but brand managers need to get involved to ensure that the voice personality goes with previously established brand characteristics. Another consideration, when companies choose a voice assistant from another company like Amazon, is to think about the user relationship. Is the user relationship going to stay with the car brand, or is the same Amazon Alexa you speak to at home now in the car? We cannot have both. , It is imperative for brand managers to understand the distinction and to make informed choices about how to appropriately bring voice into the car.

Multimodal Design Experiences

In the business setting, AIX is likely to be a multimodal experience combining multiple data sources. For example, a hospital used Tensorflow Voice API to listen to a child's voice in ICU to monitor for sounds of distress and send a mobile notification to call the parent. In this case, the application interface of the parent is on the mobile phone. The child in the hospital is a stakeholder who is interacting with the voice device. Another voice example in the hospital is a care teddy bear that the child hugs. The bear listens to the child to run a machine learning model that can predict how the child is feeling. In this case, voice input is collected and matched to pattern to categorize into multiple moods. In all of these cases, the voice design is more than just collecting voice and sending an output to some system. It requires a user-centric design with an empathy map of the users before designing the voice user interface (VUI).

A framework to design Voice User Interface (VUI) consists of three parts. The first step is to understand the user and develop a user journey map. This typically includes a **"User Persona"** in standard UX design. Personas give a personality to different kinds of users and help us get a clear picture of the user. For example, for Alexa Auto in the car, one persona is a race driver. This person may be called "Martha" and is a 35 year old racing fanatic. She loves sports and enjoys driving up mountains. Another persona could be "Aleks" who is 42 and enjoys competitive racing. Aleks enjoys driving fast and competing in cross-country races across Europe.

AIX Voice UI (VUI) Framework

INVESTIGATE	EXPLORE	DEVELOP
User Persona	Easy Path	User Flowchart
AI Persona	Wizard of Oz	Voice scripts
User journey map	test	

Sudha Jamthe (inspired by Jeff Humble, Design blogs from Alexa & Google Home)

Figure: AIX Framework to Design for Voice by Sudha Jamthe

Humanizing and Genderizing AI

In Voice UI, we define something additional that is unique. It is called **"Device Persona or AI Persona."** This is the persona of the AI. It could be Alexa Auto in the car ready to listen and help Martha or Aleks. The designer gets to define the persona of the device and humanize the AI. They get to genderize the AI, decide on a name and give them a voice as a male or female.

The Google Assistant team worked very hard to not genderize the device and to allow the user to select from various voices by picking from a visual array of colors in the mobile app. Each color then mapped to a specific voice range.

Unified Inbox gave different personalities to the same washing machine equipment by giving it different voice personality with tone of voice, quirkiness or formality in the communication, thereby helping the washing machine company make multiple products that they targeted to different age demographics.

Once you have the user and device personas, you can then draw the user journey map. This will help define the interaction map of the customer with the voice for various problems you want the Voice AI to solve.

The next step in the Voice UI design framework is to explore the voice communication between the user and the device. First design the easy path which is sure to be successful. For example, I ask Alexa, "What is the temperature outside?" and she tells me the temperature. There is no confusion of intent or context in this interaction. Next you need to develop more complex conversation voice scripts and test it with role-play within the product design team.

The final stage is to develop multiple voice scripts and develop the user flow diagram for each script. In voice, there is always the unknown of what the user's intent and interpretation of what the AI is saying. So prepare a voice script as a catch all for the indeterministic condition. Alexa says, "Sorry I cannot help you with that," when she cannot understand a user's request.

Conversational AI is the future of Voice design where the AI understands the context and is able to go past single sentence interactions to continue a human-like conversation. This is a technical challenge today with AI being developed for conversational AI. But this is also an opportunity for voice designers to get involved in innovating Voice Assistants to work for various user-centered situations.

8.2 Designing for Machine Learning (MLUX)

Machine Learning is the most commonly used AI technology. This is about classifying any data to form patterns to group customers or find anomalies or simply make a prediction on a single item. A classic example of Machine Learning is Google Search. You enter a keyword and the machine learning algorithm sifts through millions of items to find what it believes to be closest to what you are searching. Another example is your Netflix movie recommendation.

When designing AI using machine learning, the design process is again the same as the typical design process in understanding the customer and testing out an experience to get feedback to find the fit.

The difference is that with Machine Learning UX, the design is done as a two step process. As you can see from the image below, the first one stage, AI acts to augment humans in a support role. Eventually it gets fully automated.

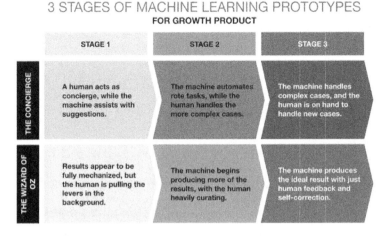

Figure: Three stages of Machine Learning Credit: Chris Butler/Reforge

Chris Butler, Machine Learning expert from Ipsoft who spoke to AIX class students on DriverlessWorldSchool.com said "With an ML prototype we're looking to get honest feedback from customers with minimum upfront investment, and without having to actually build out the entire "machine."

Machine Learning can be invisible with no UI to the user. It still will create a UX such as the perfect search results or that exact movie you want to watch next. Or it can be visible in the form with a UI displaying the right size fit in a fashion clothing all or send alerts on your mobile phone on identifying a person at the door from video footage on your security camera.

It is left to you to humanize the AI and decide what is the optimal customer experience as you take your user on a journey to enjoy the results of the prediction from machine learning algorithmic data feeds of years of past behavior.

CHAPTER 9: Designing Shared Spaces

AI is going to be in our home, our car, offices and public spaces. All of these are typically built as shared spaces with social nuances. So AI has to be designed for shared spaces.

9.1 Designing Shared In-Car Experience

A shared space brings with it the social burden of sharing a location with other people. In ride-sharing, we are sharing the car space with strangers. If the car becomes a co-working space, we bring expectations of office social relationships to the small inside space of an autonomous vehicle.

AIX

Autonomous Vehicle companies testing out Robo-Taxis, and ride-hailing services are promising to replace human drivers to get to autonomous shared-ride vehicles.

The most important business driver impacting autonomous vehicle adoption is consumer trust. But, we as people are complex beings with many emotions that affect our adoption of technology solutions. The inside of a ride-share vehicle does not adapt to the needs of introverts versus extroverts when algorithms find the best route and selects random users to ride in the car with us today. Also, as people share common space inside the car, people's dynamics of sharing the space will cause conflict and will need to be mediated by the in-car experience. For example, if Uber or Lyft is shared by a group of friends, they will expect common entertainment and the mood in the car will be one of trusting each other. If the ride is being shared by random strangers, there will be the social boundary and distrust among the riders. Also, Uber and Lyft are known to have not made the ride-sharing experience safe for women, and that requires design thinking to create the right experience, tied to policy and safety reporting changes.

As cars become autonomous in the future, the in-car experience has to be designed for different customer segments and use cases of business rides versus long distance family rides. This will require AIX based on data inside the car to offer more customized experiences.

9.2 Learn Shared Space Experience from Buildings

The good news is that we have decades of experience building shared spaces with buildings, and automating buildings is bringing us closer to a glimpse of what a shared mobility space in an AV will look like.

Office building design has adapted to the human social networks that evolve and drive our productivity, friendships, mentorships and office politics. Public buildings such as shopping malls, movie theaters, churches and temples have each evolved with their own set of social rules over the years. As buildings became automated, they first focused on the efficiency of energy-saving and digitization for security and convenience. Slowly over the years, buildings started adapting to humans. An example of this is offices switching to open spaces with kiosks for privacy allowing for the balance of introverts and extroverts to work together in a team. As Artificial Intelligence and machine learning are used in buildings to optimize for the human occupants, AI is learning the social segmentation of humans and their preferences and the right way to coexist with each other in different social constructs. We have built decades of experience of creating shared space in offices, malls, theatres, and mastered these social constructs and the many human personas. Much like we went through a process with websites and brought commerce online from offline stores, we are in infancy to bring the human social fabric from buildings to their automated AI driven presence.There is abundant opportunity for business leaders to shape this next move. Initially, website navigation was thought of as creating a new set of web design standards. Slowly it is evolving to bring social behaviour of people. So Netflix is recreating the living room by allowing users to watch movies together while physically being remote. Teens are doing social shopping by sharing pictures of clothes they try on using mobile apps.

We need to stop and look at buildings to understand what we have learned in translating human social interaction so that we can capture it and bring it elsewhere like the Autonomous Vehicle.

Why move the shared space learning from Buildings to Cars?
As we move from a building, from our home office to the car, the AI is going to go with us seamlessly. That is good and bad news. The good news is that the AI will bring the social nuances of buildings to the car and back to other buildings as it carries our mobile context with us. The bad news is that today AI is being designed for shared

experiences as if we have no learning to transfer knowledge from buildings.

When we design shared spaces for ride-sharing, we can look at office building design to see practical uses of open spaces and quiet private areas, and then try to design a similar shared experience in the car.

9.3 Designing Shared Voice Experience

Voice design has to cater to various shared space settings.
If multiple people talk at the same time, there is a machine learning algorithm called **diarization** which can separate different pitches of voice heard by the voice assistant. It is totally left to the voice designer to design the experience of whether the device should combine the voices together, or separate out the voices and listen to a particular person's voice while filtering out other voices as background noise. It all depends on the voice application and the context of interaction between the human and the voice assistant.

In the smart home, we have social nuances of privacy and intimacy that the Artificial Intelligence design has to learn, and adapt with a sensitivity that is not yet seen today in AIX design. For example, a home is a safe place for people to be authentic with all their moods and good and bad behavior. Each person in the family is going to expect their privacy protected while allowing for intimate interactions. So a voice assistant at home that listens for an invocation word to be called to fetch information from the Internet, to entertain or to give updates on weather and traffic is not a natural member of a family setting.

Recently, Google Home released a feature to ask me "How satisfied are you with this answer?" after I asked it to turn on the lights. I chose to be quiet and it went quiet too. We cannot translate user research and customer service feedback models into the design of AIX in a consumer setting, especially in a private setting such as a home. We need new models of user feedback for learning AI systems, especially for voice and for shared space experiences.

9.4 Shared Devices and Data Bullying

Today each device company is designing their customer experience thinking only about their device and the user. This is an old way of thinking from web and mobile experience where the user had their own screen. With devices becoming more prevalent, it is important to design for a world with multiple devices shared in the common space of a home, office, car or a shopping mall. When I call Google home as Alexa because I have both voice assistants in my home, Google Home corrects me and says, "That is not my name, I am your

Google Home Assistant." I tried setting a time on Google Home and right after that I set a timer on Alexa. Google Home immediately interfered in my conversation with Alexa and said "You already have a timer set for that." What is interesting in this design is that Google Home displays a sibling rivalry kind of AI personality. It is missing the point that I wanted to use both the voice assistants and setup a staggered timer because neither of them offer an snoozing option when I set a timer. So, a valuable opportunity to get my feedback as a user is lost with the Google Assistant communicating that it wants to be the only device in my home. Also, my experience of interacting with one device is now interwoven with the other irrespective of its attitude.

If this was an AR experience, with two competing options, the experience will be very confusing. So as we move forward in the connected world, it is important to design for shared spaces shared by a mix of humans and other devices.

As AI becomes more pervasive and it will be more commonly used in shared places like malls and movie theaters, airports, restaurants and offices. Then, the responsibility lies with the product designer to make voice work for the user in a shared setting. AIX for Voice will have to ensure that some users are not left behind, and that the experience reflects the problem the AI is called to solve. Only AIX for

Voice can make the AI experience natural, like a human-to-human interaction, and disarm the user to trust the AI and focus on living their lives.

Data Bullying is the problem of data being used in a shared space such as a home or office to coerce or bully another person. Designers of shared space should be aware of the ways in which the AI can be manipulated to coerce or bully someone in a shared space, plan for the non-deterministic conditions that can lead to this and then create triggers to rescue victims. For example, when designing an autonomous ride-share experience, a user must be able to report a fellow passenger who is harassing them and get help. In a smart home, will the AI allow one person to control the environment? It could be simple things such as switching off lights at a particular time or locking the door as curfew to a teenager. Offices could monitor employee movements in an effort to control them. Or in a shared room, a room mate could monitor a person by tracking their data to monitor their behaviors which could be used to bully the person. In physical design, there is a concept of fail-safe design. I participated in the Fail-Safe AI IEEE Standards Committee. Fail-safe is to design systems expecting a failure to happen at some point and to plan for a design that allows the impacted person to escape. An example of fail-safe design is for an automatic connected

Iot lock in a house to stay open in case of a fire while its job is to keep the house locked to protect the premise at all times. With AI, there should be a fail-safe design to allow for the person who is being hurt to escape when the AI is taken over by data manipulation.

Product designers in the design process usually develop personas to develop empathy for various user types. Typically for data driven AI products such as voice or video, it is common to think about privacy and security. Security is usually considered as physical security. It is important for product designers to consider a persona of a person in conflict with others sharing a common shared device experience and then figure out how that data can be used or misused.

The Power of the AI Product Manager and Designer

Khari Johnson in their article "Ethics is about Power" wrote "Power in AI is like gravity, an invisible force that influences every consideration of ethics in artificial intelligence. Power provides the means to influence which use cases are relevant; which problems are priorities; and who the tools, products, and services are made to serve." You the product designer have this power in AI to decide whether you prioritize features supporting everyone equitably. With regards to data bullying, it is easy for product managers to think it is a low priority use case even if they have experienced regular bullying out in the school playground. Data bullying is a subtle exertion of power by one person who has access to the information from a device or AI in a shared setting. For example Alexa or Google Home Voice Assistants are designed to be setup with one person's login in a shared family setting. This person has the option to setup an App to monitor usage of the Voice Assistant and set preferences. Same with home security cameras and connected doorbells monitoring the front door. This is not an issue in a healthy social environment. When there is a conflict or a distrust among partners or people sharing a home, then one person has data that they can misused or use to bully the other.

As AI becomes more prevalent and goes from home to the car to office buildings, there is more potential for this data to be used for bullying or exerting power by one person. So product designers need to be aware of their power while designing for shared experience and create a design experience which has opportunities for all involved to express their consent to data sharing. One example of this is in Google Nest Home. Everyone in the shared environment is allowed to talk to the device. Each person has the option to set up their voice to be recognized and they get special privileges. If you see a picture in a Google Nest Hub, only the person whose voice is setup is allowed to ask about where a picture shown was taken. This stops privacy invasion by random visitors to a home. This is a minor feature but a great start to offer respectful boundaries to each member in a shared space using the same device.

Design to Avoid Design Discrimination

Since AI learns continuously, every communication with the AI teaches the AI. So when an AI is deployed in a shared space or workplace, who gets to train the AI becomes important. If some group trains the AI and other groups needs are not well-represented in the training data, that could limit options and control some people. These are topics typical AI design for buildings or shared spaces in the car or public transport should consider. A product designer can achieve the right balance when they build out the AI with input from all stakeholders involved. Otherwise, very easily, this could lead to data bullying. If the AI is not trained to understand the voice accents, it will create awkward social interactions when multiple people interact with the device and it works for some and not others. For example if we use a voice assistant to turn off the lights and it does not work accurately for women, which is a bias in many AI, then the women become dependent on the men in the shared space to repeat what the women say or correct it for the device to act.

In summary, it is important for product designers to build AI to be unbiased. They also safely design it with features that are inclusive of everyone and gives options for people to consent or rescind their consent to being monitored or share their data. Designers should develop with empathy for situations where a biased AI experience will create bullying using data or socially awkward situations that targets or marginalizes some people in a group setting.

Finally a shared experience is reflective of the social constructs of the environment. So an AI design for shared spaces should plan to learn constantly to the changing social norms with feedback from customers. Today most AI we see out there are not yet designed for shared experiences and are waiting for you to pivot to AI space to design shared experiences that earns peoples' trust of the AI.

Figure: Sudha Jamthe (left) with her student Renee Manneh (right), an Autonomous Vehicle Operator.

Renee Manneh is an AV operator who brings experience driving Waymo and Voyage.auto Robotaxis in Silicon Valley. She is an example of an AI innovator who found transferable skills to pivot to AV space. She works with AI engineers to test new AI cognition software and collect training data to improve self-driving cars.

SECTION III: PIVOT

What you will learn in this section
1. When you read about AI, it comes with news about Automation and jobs replaced. Learn about what job skills are being replaced and what are the new skills needed for success in the world of AI.
2. Learn about what is unique about AI innovators, the transferable skills you bring from other industries and jobs to shape the world of AI.
3. Learn about new job roles in AI and how it fits you.

Figure: Sudha Jamthe with 'steno' robot

A robot is humanized with a gender and name by the designer. You can be that AI designer. Robots cannot replace any job. They need to be trained by business people and are being tested with mixed results on being customer service.

Chapter 10: Automation and Pivoting to AI Jobs

10.1 Job Market and Reskilling

Automation by AI replacing repeatable jobs is the biggest threat from AI. AI has begun replacing low skilled jobs and is automating many jobs that can be broken down into simple repeatable steps that an AI can learn easily. AI is redefining work as we know it and creating new jobs. People who are losing jobs to automation need skills retraining to get back into the workforce. Today, some industries are automating faster than others. The one gaining from the automation are not taking responsibility to retain the employees who are losing jobs with skills to work with AI. What is the impact of this on industries? What industries are most impacted?

Automation and Pivoting to AI

It is no secret that AI can automate many manual jobs. What is it doing to work as we know it? As a business leader, how should you view this upcoming transformation if you want to pivot your career into AI?

As you can see from the figure below, McKinsey Global Institute's Workforce Skills Model shows that jobs skills are shifting from physical labor to cognitive skills by 2030. When self-driving cars and autonomous vehicles become mainstream, they will impact truck driver jobs, public transportation and many other fields that are currently kept afloat by drivers' needs. Automation impacts customer service jobs via chatbots. AI is set to replace front end recruiters, doctors, lawyers, educators all doing repeatable jobs. Most obviously, manufacturing jobs are being replaced by robots doing the heavy lifting.

AIX

Automation and artificial intelligence will accelerate the shift in skills that the workforce needs.

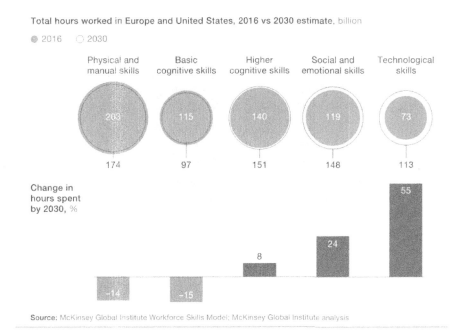

Total hours worked in Europe and United States, 2016 vs 2030 estimate, billion

● 2016   ○ 2030

Physical and manual skills	Basic cognitive skills	Higher cognitive skills	Social and emotional skills	Technological skills
203	115	140	119	73
174	97	151	148	113

Change in hours spent by 2030, %

-14   -15   8   24   55

Source: McKinsey Global Institute Workforce Skills Model; McKinsey Global Institute analysis

Figure: Mckinsey Global Workforce Analysis

I believe that in the Autonomous world when AI takes over physical work, our cognitive and empathetic skills are the only ones that will define us as humans.

AI can augment radiologists and non specialist doctors, and robots can perform precision surgery. However, robots cannot replace the empathy of a nurse. They cannot replace the kindness of teachers motivating students who feel insecure when a robot shows them where they are behind in their learning. They cannot replace the creativity of committed employees who help other work on peak workload days in any workplace.

With the industrial revolution many mechanical jobs got streamlined and automated onto a conveyor belt. But new jobs were created. As AI replaces repetitive jobs, work as we know is going to change. We see many new job functions that require integrating data into old roles. AI designers and AI product managers are two important roles in technology solutions.

As data is the language of AI by which the AI learns its purpose and communicates with its environment, data literacy will prove to be a critical skill in virtually all business enterprises. Those individuals who can find ways to monetize the use of more data in their field, will lead their respective fields as more AI gets implemented everywhere.

10.2 Pivot your career to AI

One of the biggest challenges business leaders face is retraining people who are skilled in the jobs that will become automated because of AI. One answer is to learn technology and AI development, where the number of jobs is increasing, but that is not practical and we cannot build a world with only technologists. We need skills retraining to cover a gamut of skills needed for new jobs in the world of automation.

We are at the cusp of all job roles needing to pivot to AI in their current jobs, or to make career pivots to AI Businesses. PwC says that AI Business' promised $15 Trillion will come only when business people work on AI along with technologists to tap into the power of AI to work for the overall business.

Designers have the responsibility to humanize AI. Product people need to bring their business acumen into the training data. Business people have to keep the focus on what business problems need to be solved, to drive what type of AI the company needs to build next. For example, a finance manager can decide fraud prevention will protect the assets of the company and in a siloed approach of working, this can lead to a machine learning engineer creating fraud prevention models. On the other hand if the finance manager's real need is to reduce costs from customer support calls a chatbot might help customers in an automated fashion. Or the finance person might ask for AI to detect odd patterns of customer behavior to find pain points, where to increase operational efficiencies, and the Machine Learning Engineer might build an anomaly detection system that monitors all customer data to look for outliers. So the same business person might have different business goals that apply the same customer data into different algorithms to solve their problems.

Skills Transferable to AI

The good news is that all business is becoming an AI Business. As you have read elsewhere in this book, you need business acumen and understanding of your business to apply the data from your business to transition it into an AI business. This is your opportunity to pivot to the field of AI.

Another important characteristic of AI is that unlike past technologies, AI disruption is not limited to a few industries. AI is pervasive across industries. The cascade of disruptions crosses industry value chains. For example, who would have thought Autonomous Vehicles would one day save a city from power failure and help energy companies manage demand response. Demand response is the method for energy companies to manage the fluctuating demands of customers and adjust their production or supply accordingly. Autonomous Vehicles in their effort to reduce the mile anxiety of charging for customers created 2-way batteries that can store charge. This led to V2G or Vehicle-to-Grid technology, by which a car can discharge and give charge back to the power grid. This created an opportunity for a car company such as Nissan Leaf to offer V2G service to buildings during a blackout.

So as you are looking at AI, think about what industries would benefit from your current skills, and you will find it enjoyable to work in that industry.

AI is transforming companies to be data savvy, to organize their data and find ways to operationalize efficiencies in products or processes. This leads to the digital transformation of companies and organizations. So your ability to get buy-in from multiple stakeholders, communicate your results and your ability to drive change will come in handy in any company.

Digitizing a company with AI is a test-and-learn iterative process, so being able to do quick sprints and test and validate results, and to then be able to keep moving is a very valuable skill. Being data savvy is a skill that cannot be under-rated.

All AI is doing is taking historic data and creating AI models to solve problems. So you can approach this tremendous growth opportunity by looking at the data, or by analyzing problems that AI can solve.

If your company is being disrupted by AI, there are many problems begging you to solve them. The challenge is where to focus.

According to KPMG Autonomous Vehicles Readiness Index 2019, the Netherlands is most ready for Autonomous Vehicles. This report measures readiness by current technology and consumer adoption and Government policies that protect people and jobs. AI adoption as far-reaching and impactful as Autonomous Vehicles should come with skill retraining for the people in highly impacted fields.

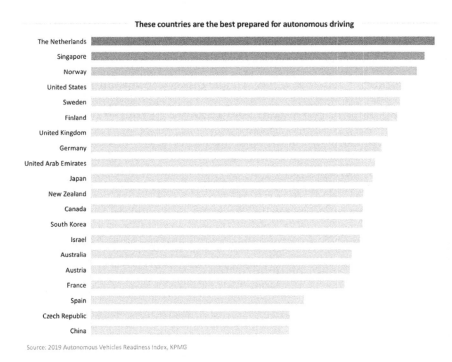

Figure: Autonomous Vehicles readiness report of countries (thanks to @RThrelfall_KPMG & team)

Oxford has an AI readiness index of Governments compiled by Oxford Insights and the International Development Research Centre.

Another approach is to find transferable skills that you utilize to change an existing product or process into an AI product or process.

One common challenge business people face in pivoting to AI is

their lacking technical skills.

AI is one technology that is easier to learn than past technologies because it does not require that you learn programming. What you need a solid understanding of data and how algorithms work.

There is no company or city in the whole world who has a handle on what data they have and how they are organized. So start by developing an understanding of what data exists in your company or city, and what role it plays in your company. The world of possibilities may not be readily visible. . The next step is to look at customer problems. What customer problem can you solve using data? Find that data and who owns it, and then determine how to clean and organize this data. Then contemplate what AI can do to help solve the problem. Is it about predicting or forecasting, or personalizing, or recommending?

The other factors you should look at are what stage of AI adoption is your organization going through. Are there some parts of the organization more advanced than others? What is your customer readiness? Is the customer savvy about how AI can help them? Is competition doing something with AI that is attracting customers towards them? Is your company at the center of the industry shift to AI? Eg. Dealers impacted by Autonomous Vehicles

Once you have an understanding of the specific customer problems you want to solve and what data assets you have in the company, the next step is to carve out pilot AI application projects you can start testing. . This is the fastest way to pivot within a company. This will help you develop the learning, get some experience and go through the path to understand which of your past experiences are transferable to AI.

10.3 Your Role in Automating Jobs in Your Company

It is an interesting perspective to question whether an employee owns their knowledge or HAS to transfer it to an AI when their job area gets automated. Knowledge is not just the technical know-how to do a job. In the same company, people establish trust that they can get a job done faster or with better quality with their own resourceful ways over the years. Such a person is paid a salary for their job (like any other employee). But the employee who can execute efficiently and reliably gets better projects, or gets hired by the boss when they move to a new company or role. This is an intangible that is being overlooked when we ask employees to transfer their jobs to an AI. It is similar to asking a reluctant employee to transfer their job to another person when they leave. AI is learning the learned skills and methods. It is not going to be able to transfer best practices, or good processes that are part of a company's DNA. I wonder if there could be an economic incentive model created to create that partnership between an employee and AI to get this transfer willingly with respect?

Companies own employees inventions and creative ideas to solve problems while doing their job. But it is more nuanced than that when you think about what knowledge a long term employee has in a particular business. People who stay within one industry have business acumen. Long term employees have knowledge gathered over year about the culture, processes and dna of the company to know what method gets the job done. How do you capture this in an AI training dataset? I'd take it further to employees who are top performers who have accumulated knowledge over a career beyond one job where they bring experience, passion and expertise to solve problems intuitively. You can quantify the expertise but not their secret sauce stemming from experience and passion. So when an employee trains and AI to do their job, it is like an experienced teacher of many decades teaching only technique to a toddler.

10.4 AI Product Managers & AI Designers

AI Product Managers and Training the AI

The role of the Product Manager is a pivotal role in Technology. Product Managers build the product flows and optimal integration points. They are necessary to adapt to how artificial intelligence changes the product's interaction with customers and create new customer segments and price sentiments. Technology product managers and domain expert business managers from Automotive and Transportation industries came to learn about autonomous vehicle technology, and changing customer demands to fill these new Product Manager roles.

The biggest job of a product manager is to provide the training data. They have to be the CEO of the business in looking out for the customer while keeping the balance of business growth balanced against the interest of all other stakeholders. They have to make sure that the training data is reflective of the business acumen that resides in the company.

AI can be incorporated in new products or extend a product line such as Amazon Echo is doing. They will have to integrate one product into another such as Nest and Google Home become Google Home Hub. They will have to use AI to drive process change such as being done in autonomous truck companies in the retail supply chain by Nuro. The product manager gets to design the training data and fill in gaps known as '**ML Optimization**' which are gaps that reflect business situations but are not available in the data. They get to take ownership for the success of the AI and its business impact to keep the balance between engineers and business leaders hungry to digitize and innovate using AI.

AI Designers

The AI designer is the evolution of UX and UI designers as they adapt to designing AI working with data feeds. An AI designer still has to follow the standard design process of working on user research, defining user personas and creating user journey maps and empathy maps and iterating to come up with the right design and test it out to find what best suits the customer and the overall business needs. What is different is the power an AI designer yields unlike other AI roles. The designer gets to humanize the AI. The designer gets to generalize the AI by creating a device personality. Try talking to Google Home and Alexa Voice assistants in the same room and they will each give snarky comments when they hear the other one's name mentioned. This is not accidental and a thoughtful design of each of the voice designers. Why are robots male and assistants female? The AI designer needs to own their new roles to ensure that we do not build out digitized systems as computers carrying the biases of the makers but are designed with human computer interface, ethically and work to earn the trust of the customer.

Figure: (left)My student Michelle Kyrouz, Host, Smarter Cars Podcast

SECTION IV: TRANSFORM

What you will learn in this section
1. What are the top three industries disrupted by AI?
2. Learn about Digital Mobility and Autonomous Vehicles AI
3. Learn about Digital Health & Sustainability and where you can innovate

Chapter 11: TOP AI DISRUPTIONS

We cannot look at AI as yet another technology wave. It is
pervasive.

Some people hear the term "Artificial Intelligence," and get all
bug-eyed at the thought of George Orwell's 1984 becoming a
reality. Others scoff, thinking it is far-fetched, or that it won't be
nearly as impactful as the hype predicts. The term itself is
super-charged.

As a cutting edge business leader, your task is to demystify AI for
others and to help them understand what it means to use data to
train an algorithm to solve a problem. "Machine Learning," it must
be understood, really refers to humans feeding data to a computer
(i.e. Machine), to fine tune an algorithm, so that it gets more
efficient at doing what that human wants it to do (i.e. it Learns). As
developers get better at using AIX, and as users get better at
iterating the systems, AI will become more and more powerful, and
more prevalent. It has already begun to change the way we live our
lives, the way business gets conducted and the way people interact

with machines. Particularly, I focus on three areas of impact and will cover them in-depth in this section.

11.1 Digital Mobility

AI with its promise of autonomous vehicles is changing how we move from home to work or travel long distance in a connected, sustainable world with shared and micro-mobility. This is powered by data training car cognition using Computer Vision and mobility data that is shifting from the mobile to the car, carrying our context and intent with us crossing geographies and disrupting many industries including Automotive, Transportation, Logistics, Retail, Healthcare, Entertainment, Real Estate, and more.

11.2 Digital Health

AI with its predictive power is feeding on medical data from wearables, medical records and digitized images of disease patterns to change how we take care of our health from being reactive to predictive. This impacts healthcare, insurance, pharmaceuticals, Hospitals, and creates a cascade effect on other industries by increasing human lifespans and quality of lives.

11.3 AI for Good

AI for Good has the potential to solve all 17 United Nations Sustainability Goals from zero hunger to climate action. Wind farms are already being monitored using machine learning to predict optimization by looking at large volume of weather feeds. AI is used in agriculture to reduce food shortage. AI is used in predicting and tackling the changing weather patterns with climate change. AI is automating everything we do and every possible product and process in industry. We hear about bias in AI data because of the training data used to train the AI. I believe that we are seeing biases because AI in its path to automate everything is just reflecting our biases as humans. It is reflecting the racism, sexism and social inequality that exists today. So by automating our world with AI and people becoming aware of these inequalities, we have an opportunity to fix them making our world better for all of us. That is my aspiration on the real power of AI to do good for all mankind.

Now let us look at the top three areas where AI is making the biggest difference for human life.

Chapter 12: DIGITAL MOBILITY

12.1 AI in the Autonomous Vehicle

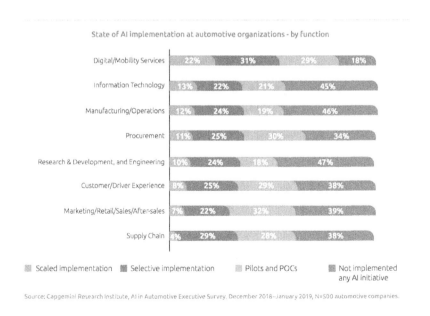

State of AI implementation at automotive organizations - by function

Digital/Mobility Services: 22% | 31% | 29% | 18%
Information Technology: 13% | 22% | 21% | 45%
Manufacturing/Operations: 12% | 24% | 19% | 46%
Procurement: 11% | 25% | 30% | 34%
Research & Development, and Engineering: 10% | 24% | 18% | 47%
Customer/Driver Experience: 8% | 25% | 29% | 38%
Marketing/Retail/Sales/After-sales: 7% | 22% | 32% | 39%
Supply Chain: 4% | 29% | 28% | 38%

Scaled implementation ▪ Selective implementation ▪ Pilots and POCs ▪ Not implemented any AI initiative

Source: Capgemini Research Institute, AI in Automotive Executive Survey, December 2018–January 2019, N=500 automotive companies.

Figure: Capgemini Research Institute, AI in Automotive Executive

SUDHA JAMTHE

Survey

The autonomous vehicle is not solely about making our cars and trucks drive themselves without a human driver. It is a fundamental shift in urban mobility as we've known it for 100 years.

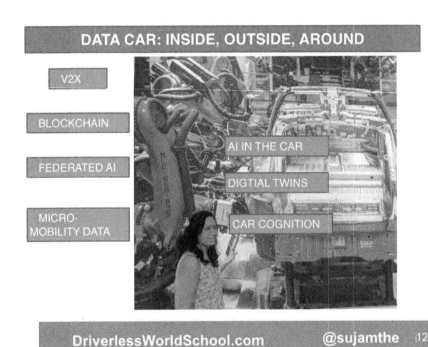

Figure: Variety of data in the Car, Sudha Jamthe

As the figure shows, there is data inside the car from the various sensors tracking the health of various car parts, known as digital twins. There is data moving from the car to the city infrastructure, to other cars and to remote dealer networks, known as Vehicle to Vehicle or Vehicle to Infrastructure communication, commonly referred as V2X. Micro mobility data refers to data from shared bikes that could interact with autonomous vehicles. We will cover Federated AI in a later chapter. Below, there are details about specific AI technologies collectively known as "car cognition" that help the car see the road, manage obstacles and drive autonomously .

Lane Detector – This is a software module that helps the car identify lanes on the road. In lane detection, the computer identifies where the lanes are on the road at any given moment. The car uses this information to stay within the lanes. It is very difficult to build models for lane detection, due to different road conditions, weather conditions, different types of lanes, lane shadows or missing lanes. It gets tricky when the road curves and there are other objects such as dividers and walls on the edges of the roads.

Early stages of development of lane detection technology were done using Computer Vision, a technology that helped computers collect, interpret and make decisions based on frames of images or videos. Deep Learning has replaced this by feeding videos of several real roads to the self-driving car to train it in lane detection with a high degree of accuracy.

Image Credit: Shirish Jamthe's open source Computer Vision lane detection model. This picture shows what a self-driving car sees as the lane and the curvature of the road. It uses this to decide how much to turn its steering wheels to stay within the lane.

Using the lanes detected, the car makes constant calculations of how much to turn the steering wheel to stay within its lane as it navigates the road ahead.

Objection Detection – Traffic signs, Road signs & Obstacles

The autonomous vehicle learns to identify traffic signs using Image recognition and Object identification, both of which apply machine learning technology. A computer model is trained on a large computer with a powerful GPU in the cloud, with thousands of images of road signs in all conditions of wear and tear, light conditions and viewing angles as training data. Next, it is trained on Object identification to read posted road speeds and other words on the road signs. These create the models that are stored in the car's software. These models help the car identify road signs and what they mean. When the car sees an object on the road, its software uses the models it has onboard to run a prediction and to decide whether it is approaching a traffic sign or a road sign, or an obstacle. This predictive module of the car is the Object detection module software.

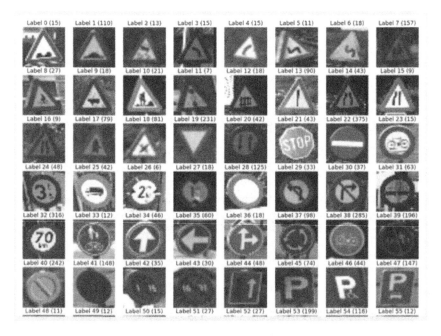

Image Credit: Waleed Abdulla's open source traffic sign recognition software model. This shows how the car sees the different traffic sign images and learns to identify road signs.

This same object detection technology is used to identify other objects on the road. Another car or a pedestrian are both treated as objects by the Driverless car. It uses Deep Learning to teach the car to identify objects on the road. Deep Learning is an advanced technology, next step to Machine Learning, where the computer takes a lot of training data, and figures out what the different objects and patterns are without any person guiding what signals the computer should look for in the data. This removes the limitation of what signals a human might expect the computer to learn in the training data. For example, when a person sees a scene they observe many things and recall different objects as being similar to other objects they may have seen before. This is how the human brain identifies things even when presented in various contexts.

For example, instead of identifying a 70-mph traffic sign as an image with a directive, humans learn numbers and identify 7 and 0 anywhere they see them together as "70." They learn traffic signs as being a particular shape and size and expect to see them in certain parts of the road at a certain height. So when they see the traffic speed limit sign, they identify it naturally without any ambiguity. Neural networks allow the computer using deep learning to learn an environment similarly. This is applied to object detection in driverless car technology to enable the car to identify the signs independent of their angle, wear and tear and any weather damage, naturally with a close to a human-like cognition of objects.

Image Credit: Shirish Jamthe's open source Deep Learning neural network model identifying vehicles. This is how self-driving cars will see other cars.

Predicting other cars and people

Autonomous cars have a prediction algorithm that uses all of the information about the objects in the road and their speed and positions to predict their actions. Tesla cars have developed what they call a fleet's "learning ability." Tesla collects data from its fleet of operating cars, including those driven by humans, crossing a GPS location to create a map of the driving world and make note of driver behavior at certain locations. It applies machine learning and uses this information as training data to create models to be used by future Tesla cars. They use this model with real time road conditions and objects to make predictions about the movement of other cars on the road. A Tesla in autopilot mode will apply a mild brake even if their optical cameras do not see an obstruction, based on the knowledge gathered from their fleet's learning ability model.

Tesla Model S and Model X have 10,000 cars with radars that drivers switch to autopilot, their autonomous driving mode. These cars send millions of GB of data to the Tesla cloud daily. Tesla uses this as training data to fine tune their autonomous vehicle software technology. Tesla develops predictive algorithms that the car can use to watch for behaviors of other cars on the road. One Tesla predicted an accident two cars ahead and took immediate action to save the Tesla car and driver. It is important to note that this learning is not happening in real time in the car. The company continues to improve its car software model, as it receives more new data from various driving scenarios, but it is important to note that the individual cars will not benefit from the new data until the company pushes out a software update. This is where the next model, OTA comes in.

Algorithm to Make Driving Decisions

The car has a real-time operating system, which it uses to apply the models it has learned and make decisions to accelerate, stop or turn at every point in the road. The car makes continuous decisions to keep it driving down the road safely and efficiently. Though it might seem like a simple software that the car will machine learn, there are boundary conditions that determine how the car will make moral decisions in rare situations where it has to decide to stop or proceed between two risky situations that might kill a human. We will talk about this moral dilemma later in the book. Today, there is no transparency on what these boundary conditions are and how the driverless car software is programmed for the available autonomous vehicle pilots on the road.

V2V communication

In 2017, the US government mandated driverless car companies to share their data to help each other be aware of the intent of other driverless cars. This is called V2V communication. V2V was a new concept in 2017, with no standards on what this data was going to be. Companies are getting ready to share the minimum data mandated by the government. I believe that they are planning on building their own predictive algorithms to give them a competitive edge in developing the best self-driving car. Today, there is no technology to facilitate the sharing of data between human driven cars and driverless cars.

Healing AI and Disengagement self-checks

These are pieces of software baked into the brains of a self-driving car that continually checks to see if there are any risky conditions that require disengaging from self-drive mode (during the phase when self-driving cars still had a standard driver ready to take control). This served as an alert module for the car to self-check whether it hits any boundaries of its autonomous learning capabilities to avoid crashes. In March 2017, Uber shocked the world with its disengagement report that showed that the self-driving car was taken over by the human driver every mile on average. Each of these was an opportunity for Uber to improve the self-driving car software.

Oliver Cameron @olivercameron · Oct 24
Just submitted my first @udacity self-driving car project! Featuring Canny edge detection, Hough transforms and more. Let's hope I pass! 😬

↩ 10   ↻ 24   ♥ 131   •••

Image Credit: Sudha Jamthe. Picture shows tweet by Oliver Cameron, then VP Engineering and Product at Udacity (now CEO of Voyage) showing what a self-driving car sees as lanes on the road.

Can AI help us to get to level 5?

Imitation learning and Reinforced learning are two techniques that show promise in improving car cognition to get self-driving cars to level 5, where they can drive better than any human without the need for a human to monitor them in all road conditions.

12.2 Mobility Services

The data in the connected cars offered a wealth of options for Car Manufacturers (OEMs) and several technology start-ups to build out AI to offer personalized mobility services.

Mobility as a Service (MAAS) is a mobility service offering that helps connected vehicle users with new conveniences, based on precious data about the car and the user. After-sales-service will change to a predictive model where the car informs the service shop when it needs maintenance and proactively schedules itself for maintenance. The autonomous vehicle will drive itself for service, adapting to the work schedule of its human passenger.

OEMs could offer Infotainment and digital streaming services with an awareness of the human passenger's needs as the car drives the user to their multiple destinations. Each usage of the car provides data about the user's behavior and mobility patterns, creating a wealth of service using personalization with recommendation algorithms. For example, an autonomous vehicle collects data and knows the regular timings that a user commutes to work and their habits to stop at certain destinations or follow certain routes. They know when the user uses the vehicle for entertainment or for work. This can enable an AI model to develop personalization, using a recommendation AI, and offer mobility services that are personalized to the user, saving them money and time.

As the car develops more cognition with the car AI, it can learn the user's emotional response to geo-fencing deals and various stimuli in their infotainment needs. All of this gives room to a broad range of mobility services.

When cars begin to use Blockchain technologies, it gives more options for mobility service because cars could make payments for a user's services based on a trusted distributed ledger. For example, an autonomous vehicle could offer to self-park after dropping off the user and then pay for its parking service using Blockchain. The car could become smarter about available parking spaces and best cost by negotiating with other cars and parking garages remotely. We will cover AI and Blockchain later in the book when we talk about Open AI and open data to democratize data.

Innovation in Mobility Services is a huge opportunity equally available to Auto OEMs and businesses big and small.

Today most new cars are made with some form of connectivity using a SIM card, though this is not exposed to the customer. Cars are created with digital twins which are their digital replica. These digital twins reside in the cloud or remote locations. Connected Vehicles send data from car parts and their digital twins to the cloud.

12.3 AI in Retail for Mobility

The promise of autonomous vehicles has initiated the technology stack from mobile to the car, using a mobile app as an intermediary stage. Many OEMs are building native mobility platforms in the car. Google Android and Apple iCar are offering connectivity via mobile phones. Amazon Auto has brought voice to the car. All of this creates data in the car. This data carries consumer context to the car as users move from home or work. For example, a consumer may continue a work call from home into the car as they head out in the morning. Another consumer may be leaving work and heading to a celebration for a special occasion. Each person's context carries from their phones to the car. The connected car now has the opportunity to serve the user with mobility services in the car or from a third party provider as the car takes the user mobile.

AI in mobility is not always in the car. It increasingly allows a car to interact with retail or other real estate structures such as parking garages and city infrastructures such as traffic lights. Retailers are beginning to take advantage of the vast customer data they have in-house to use AI to offer personalized experiences for the mobility customer. They are not yet offering in-car services that utilizes the data of the user in the car.

12.4 Contextual Real-Time Insurance

By the end of 2017, insurance companies with usage-based insurance gave drivers a 2-inch dongle device to plug into their car's dashboard to collect location and driving data. TomTom's Coordina, Metromile Pulse from Mobile Devices of France, and Progressive's Snapshop are dongle based insurance vendors. They collected driving behavior data, and built accurate risk models to adjust insurance premiums. They could collect real-time data about the driving behavior of the driver and could build accurate risk models to adjust insurance premiums. GE built this type of dongle into cars in 2017, to collect driving behavior data, but offered it as a choice, so the driver could opt into sharing this with insurance companies.

Cars have data on actual driving behavior tied to time and location. In 2017, this was not easy to export out of the vehicles. As autonomous vehicles became more prevalent, insurance companies began to use this data. Over the years with autonomous vehicles, this began to be used to make claims and disputes accurate, saving valuable time.

Contextual real-time insurance is on the verge of becoming a reality. Car AI can now help determine who was responsible for the insurance coverage in real-time. Here is an example of the contextual switch of real-time coverage from Michael Conner, CEO of Silicon Valley Insurance Accelerator (SVIA). With a fleet of driverless vans, the owner of the fleet is responsible for insurance when the van is loaded correctly and doing a delivery. If the user of the vehicle does not load it correctly or negligently uses it in hazardous areas known for vandalism, the responsibility switched to the user of the van. If some sensors on the van were not functioning properly, while driving autonomously, the van responsibility shifted to the van maker. If the user decides to switch out of autonomous mode and drives the vehicle manually, in some situations, she bears the responsibility of the insurance.

The consumers had to trade off insurance premiums for the privacy of their driving data. Insurance companies wanted to make this a positive experience for their customers.

Over the next decade, wearables on the commuters' body began to communicate with the Car AI. There was the looming possibility that these wearables could be nanobots swimming inside a human body or an implant that enhanced their brain. Either way, they offered data about the people inside the car. When car communication becomes more prevalent, the car AI could communicate with the human's data.

Keeping the user experience be at the heart of their business, insurance companies should use the AI experience to transform previously negative discussions with their customers to acting more like a life coach, guiding users' risk choices based on data from the auto and other IoT devices.

Chapter 13: DIGITAL HEALTH

When you visited the doctor the last time, do you remember meeting her AI helper? No, I don't remember either. But guess what, AI is looking at our biometrics, and combing through millions of gigabytes of past patient history and medical research papers to make predictions about our health.

Read on, regardless of whether you are a healthcare provider, or whether you work in a hospital, in a clinic, at a health insurer or at a pharmaceutical company, or whether you are an entrepreneur aspiring to bring AI to any of these industries.

Value from healthcare data

Hospitals in just the U.S. are losing up to $300 billion yearly from the lost opportunity of creating value with their healthcare data.

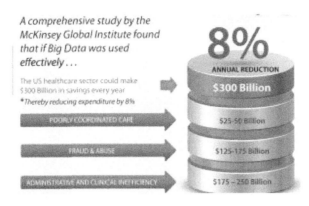

Healthcare data has grown so much that they coined the term, "yottabytes," one of which is equivalent to 2^{80} bytes.

Artificial Intelligence technologies are beginning to be employed on healthcare data to make sense of patterns of fraud, improve clinical inefficiencies and coordinate care processes to reduce healthcare costs by 80%.

Significant AI disruption in healthcare has begun.

13.1 Top AI disruptions in healthcare

Connected hospitals with intelligent messaging

In today's hospitals, pacemakers, defibrillators and oximeters are all connected to the internet and share vitals immediately with doctors, in turn speeding response times. Hospitals have technicians, nurses, staff, billing departments, insurance providers, patients and patients' families as stakeholders, each with different information requirements related to the care given to the patient.

Unified Inbox offers an AI-based unified cloud IoT messaging platform for internet of things devices to connect various stakeholders, giving them the freedom to receive different messages at different frequency, with different senses of urgency in different mediums of their choice. Unified Inbox launched this at Nanyang Polytechnic in Singapore as "CUBE," the IoT-secure messaging gateway for healthcare. The artificial intelligence makes the hospitals connected, giving peace of mind to patients and their loved ones while improving efficiency in the overall hospital management and interaction with all stakeholders.

Drones as a service

Artificial Intelligence is used in the form of machine learning and computer vision to train drones to drive autonomously. Drones are now deployed as a service and have begun disrupting the healthcare industry.

Zipline makes a drone that delivers medical supplies in Rwanda. Delft University in the Netherlands has piloted the Ambulance Drone, which can drive autonomously to an emergency site on-demand and will act as the eyes of remote emergency personnel while also acting as a connected defibrillator.

13.2 Robotic Haptic Feedback Toys and Robotic Surgery

Robots are driven using artificial intelligence. BigAu makes robots in the form of toys for kids in long-term care in hospitals. BigAu uses IBM Watson's AI technology to teach the robot biomimicry social skills to collect information about how the child is feeling from biometrics and haptic feedback to get optimal care for the child.

Robotic surgery is another area where robots are used to perform remote surgery with a skilled surgeon at a console in the operating room, manipulating the wristed robotic instruments in real-time. DaVinci Surgical Systems from Intuitive Surgical has performed robotic surgery on three million patients. Robots are not only used for remote access, but also for precision during the surgery.

in Feb 2020, Medtronics, has acquired Digital Surgery, a London-based AI company for the operating room. "As we have been approaching the commercialization of our robotics platform, we've been, in parallel, focused on investing in and developing products, road maps and capabilities in those vectors," said Megan Rosengarten, vice president and general manager of Medtronic's surgical robotics business. The four vectors Rosengarten refers to are visualization and navigation, instrumentation and implants, data and analytics, and the robotics platforms, part of Medtronics CEO stated vision to apply computer-guided surgery and planning tools to multiple medical specialties, including bringing robotics to bear on virtually every area the company has a procedural presence.

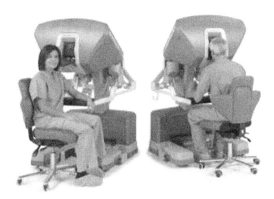

Figure: Intuitive Surgical DaVinci Surgical System being used by doctors.

Robotic arms are also being developed to act as prosthetic arms for disabled patients. With the help of AI, they allow the patient to move the robotic arm using their mind by mapping the electric pulses from their thoughts.

Deep learning algorithms

AI algorithms can comb through large volumes of patient data to look for patterns to make a personalized prediction about whether a patient is likely to get certain diseases. DeepMind, a Google company, has partnered with NHS in the UK with an app called

Streams to apply deep learning AI algorithms to patient data to predict kidney failures or eye problems before they occur. DeepMind also uses AI to help doctors separate out cancer cells from non-cancer cells for radiation therapy.

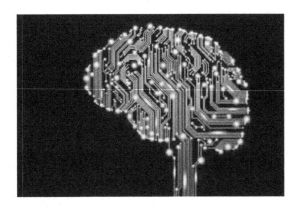

IBM Watson AI took 10 minutes to comb through 20 million cancer research papers, and helped a patient in Japan get the right treatment by spotting a rare type of leukemia. IBM Watson has partnered with Memorial Sloan Kettering Cancer Center and created Watson Oncology to augment the physician's experience to identify the type of cancer in patients. IBM has made this AI available for their employees and their families fighting cancer starting in January 2017.

AI is here to save lives now!

13.3 Nanobots: Wearables Inside Us

Wearables are becoming available as pills to swim inside our bodies. This seems far-fetched, but the applications from such pills are also equally amazing.

Proteus offers a FDA approved pill that can track our biometrics from inside our bodies. Nanobots are tiny devices that swim inside our body and share pictures of our cells. This creates a huge volume of images, which are processed by artificial intelligence using machine learning to identify cancer cells. The nanobots can then be used to kill the cancer cells.

Which AI innovation will disrupt the world?

Which of these AI disruptions do you think will change the world of medicine, extend life and change our interaction with intelligent machines? Which AI do you see disrupting your industry? Where do you see the opportunity? Do you see any challenges for your industry?

I am excited to meet my doctors' AI helper soon. Are you?

CHAPTER 14: SUSTAINABILITY

As you pivot your career into the exciting world of AI, you have the opportunity to make an impact on the world on an unprecedented scale that is not possible with any other technologies.

Standard's Institute for Human Centered Artificial Intelligence has identified the key factors that affect AI for social good.

Figure: Stanford HAI AI Vibracy Factors affecting AI for social good

The good news is that AI is able to meet all 17 sustainability goals set forth in the UN. McKinsey has done extensive research on this and arrived at 165 use cases of AI that span across multiple industries and meet the UN Sustainability goals.

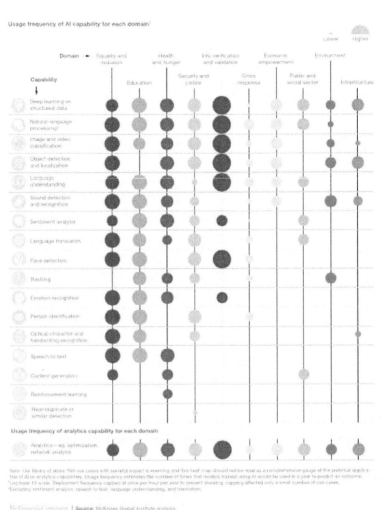

Figure: McKinsey analysis of AI for UN's 17 Sustainability goals

SECTION II: IMPACT

<u>What you will learn in this section</u>

1. Do you want to learn how to impact the world of AI? Learn where you can make an impact and what are the immediate opportunities and what are futuristic opportunities.

2. Have you thought about how we go from buildings to buildings from home to office to shopping mall or hospitals or movie theater and drive or fly or take public transport in between them? Learn about AI carrying our context from automated buildings to the car and how this is going to change how we live in the future.

3. If AI is so pervasive impacting all walks of life, we need to build it as an open technology. Find out about Open AI. Learn about Federated AI, the concept of building distributed machine learning between companies. Finally, we will cover a very important topic, ethics in AI. FInd out how ethics in AI impacts lives and how you have the power and responsibility to build AI ethically.

Figure: Jason Marks, my student, Autonomous Vehicle Business Development Manager, National Semiconductor and ceo Olley.io. Jason is a role model for engineers who can transition to client facing roles and become AV entrepreneurs.

Chapter 15: Autonomous Buildings

What are Intelligent Buildings?

Buildings may be constant structures, but the cascade of disruptions on automated building stakeholders is definitely evolving for the better to create efficiencies and new ways of living and managing the property.

In the world of Technology Disruptions, buildings are one constant structure where we live, work, shop or sleep. When the building is a home, it comes with amenities to create conveniences and make us feel safe. When the building is a factory or office building, the focus is on efficiency and keeping people who work there productive. When it is a retail building, the focus shifts to the experience of the retail customer. In hospitals and multi-tenant buildings, the complexity increases to serve multiple stakeholders while still keeping the cost down.

How do all these different types of buildings become smart? Buildings and the appliances and equipment inside are becoming connected with sensors that speak to the Internet. These sensors produce a large volume of data about the health of the building structure, the safety of the environment, the efficiency of energy usage and the operational usage of the building assets by various stakeholders. Artificial Intelligence can take advantage of this data to make buildings safer and more efficient. This data becomes the training data to build AI models to design the end to end experience of users of building. For example, sensor data about energy usage can help building managers manage heat setting of the building on cold days. Data about what parts of the building has increased usage can train AI models to make proactive predictions to help building managers manage maintenance schedules

What does a smart building do?

A smart home keeps us safe and comfortable. A smart factory or commercial building should run efficiently and safely, and create conveniences for the occupants, facilities managers, building owners and all stakeholders.

So at a minimum, you can start looking at buildings to do the following:

1. Energy efficiency
2. Safety management

3. Compliance to building code and other regulations such as fire code

Introducing Intelligent Buildings

An intelligent building with AI will do all of the above plus solve problems that current buildings cannot, by adding convenience for facility managers, occupants, building supply makers and building owners.

Today, facility managers can use mobile apps while they are on vacation to remotely look at a dashboard of data showing how their buildings are performing or click to do simple operations that need their authorization.

AI in the form of machine learning takes it a step further by making buildings intelligent. The following examples show how stakeholders can achieve new goals in the Automated Building value chain:

1. Energy management of buildings using Predictive Models

Appliance or equipment energy management machine learning models help reduce energy consumption. Figure 1 below shows the Machine Learning model for residential appliance energy consumption.

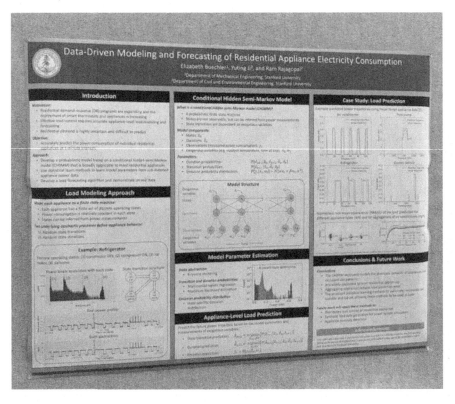

Figure: Machine Learning model from Stanford Civil and Environment Engineering and Stanford Mechanical Engineering Department Students at Stanford Energy Week Poster session. Machine Learning helps offer a spatial and temporal model of urban building energy consumption. See Figure 2 for the model developed by the Student team at Stanford Urban Informatics Lab as seen in the poster at Stanford Energy Week 2019.

Figure:: Machine Learning model for Urban Building Energy Usage from Stanford Urban Information Lab.

2. Sustainable energy management

Electric vehicle charging stations are becoming more common in various types of buildings, including residential, commercial and industrial. Machine Learning (ML) models can predict the load on the utility grid to manage demand response. See Figure 3 for a forecasting model developed by students using PECAN data set tracking EV usage in a residential community in Austin, Texas.

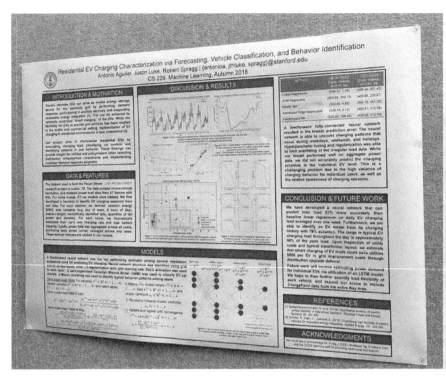

Figure 3: Forecasting model of EV Utilization from Public Austin City PECAN data set.

3. Microgrids and sustainable battery storage utilization

Companies are building machine learning models to take meter data and predict loads to manage the charge and discharge of batteries to save energy costs for buildings.

Enel X, the green tech unit of Italian utility Enel has taken it one step further. They take smart meter data from EVs, Buildings, Solar and process this in real time to manage the energy storage and utilization for buildings.

Biometrics for Building Security

Security cameras watch building entrances, apply machine learning to identify people through facial recognition and then track who enters, to increase building security. Fingerprinting is used commonly to identify people authorized to enter buildings.

Figure 4: Fingerprinting for employee identification at 'Letgo' offices in Barcelona, Spain. Credit: Sudha Jamthe

5. Robots and Drones

Robots come in many forms in smart buildings. Knightscope Robots watch the periphery of buildings at Google and Juniper to augment the building security. They use AI, Anomaly detection to look out for abnormal patterns to alert the security team. See Figure 5 for the security robot.

Drones are used in buildings for aerial photography and surveying. In 2018, drones seen flying near airports caused flights to be cancelled at Heathrow airport creating security fears. So drones flying in buildings are going to require more security checks before they can be deployed easily. AI in buildings is easier to adapt to using AI algorithms than physical robots and drones.

Buildings of all kinds will benefit from energy saving, operational efficiency and create new convenience for all stakeholders by adopting Artificial Intelligence. Artificial Intelligence today comes in the form of Machine Learning algorithms using public urban data, EV car charging data and private usage data of appliances and meters in buildings.

Collision of Autonomous Vehicles and Autonomous Buildings

Buildings may be constant structures, but the cascade of disruptions on automated building stakeholders is definitely evolving for the better to create efficiencies and new ways of living and managing the property as we get to the connected Driverless World. Autonomous Automated Buildings and autonomous vehicles are on a collision course as cities get smart or digitized.

What is a City?

It is generally assumed that it is a physical geographical area with buildings and some nature - trees, beaches, rivers, mountains etc. What does it mean for us to identify with a city? We call a place our home town. We were born or grew up for a substantial part of our early formative years and have memories and our early identity tied to that place.

Many of us live in one city or town and commute to work in another. We develop an affinity to the place we work as we create memories of spending time with colleagues and growing up in their careers, developing a part of our professional identities there.

Today, people work remotely, and travel occasionally to visit other work locations to meet colleagues with whom they work remotely using some technology. As the book, *workism* says, globally spread out companies are giving a sense of purpose, community and identity to employees and is becoming the equivalent of religion.

So there's the home town where one's identity is shaped and is more amorphous than real. There's the work city where we commute daily and spend money on lunch at restaurants, parking, maybe grocery, salons as we shop on our way out of work. Then, there is our relationship with the extended web of cities we visit that is tied to our identity of work and work relationships. *So cities are essentially places we spend time in, and it contributes to our relationships with people who share the same physical space with us and contributes to our identity in some form.*

What Shifts when Cities Become Smart?

Now, in this context, let us think of making our cities smart. The word smart seems to imply that what we have is dumb so I don't like that term.

Digitizing our cities to automate them to make life better for the users (residents, visitors).

The first step to digitizing the city is digitizing the infrastructure, adding Internet of Things sensors and connectivity to add efficiency to manage city resources such as water, waste, energy and real-estate such as parks, bridges, and buildings. The second step is to digitize the residents' communication with the city in the form of city hall online and tools for residents' communication with the city leaders and amongst themselves or non-profit organizations.nAll this still keeps the city as a fixed physical space centered around main street and city hall with citizens as spokes to a fixed system tied to separate industries.

Real civic automation occurs when buses, trains, ride-sharing and AVs get digitized, disrupting traditional modes of transportation. It gives residents increased power and aids the influx of visitors who travel about the city for business and recreation.

When people can be mobile when they work, coffee shops are not just for coffee but become meeting places for business and remote workplaces for people working with companies outside the city. When people can manage their mobility seamlessly with connectivity everywhere, they care less about the space they use to meet or work and extend that to their cars or trains.

Smart Cities to Automated Intelligence

The next step to this automation is intelligence in the buildings, in the mobility infrastructure with a digital identity that can move with people. Mobility data of people's transactional mobility needs of going between home and work or preferred coffee shop drop-offs by a ride-share company or their preference when to hail a taxi vs pickup an e-mobility bike becomes the fuel that powers this intelligence.

Now, I want you to stop and think about why this intelligence should be different in buildings, separate from the mobility vehicle when the user blurs the line between them and is focused on working or living their lives.

Now add to that the complexity that each person has their own preference of time, location and preferred mobility and workspace channels that they want to be personalized to them. For example someone is a morning person and works till their kid comes home at 3pm when they go pick them up while someone else preferred to work during the whole day and enjoy the evening with family or friends.

The mobility data that powers this lifestyle essentially extends the boundary of cities for people and is the key driver that brings the collision of buildings and vehicles as conjoint spaces serving the needs of the people.

Now let us go back to that topic we started with about what defines a city and how the identity of the person is developed in their hometown, the city where they work and extended cities they visit. What is the shift in the identity of the person as they blur the boundary of the working space aka building and mobility vehicle? That shift of identity, I believe, is going to shift from the city to the autonomous vehicles. This is where the automated building is on a collision path with autonomous vehicles.

We should not think of where the person spends their time. But let us think about it as what experience of interacting with the data and AI builds trusts and binds the identity of people, so they willingly share data of who they become as mobile working and mobile living beings.

It is time we stop focusing on automating buildings or vehicles for efficiency and begin focusing on the experience we give people with AIX or AIxDesign to seamlessly move between buildings and vehicles to expand their worlds to a more joyful place.

For AIX to work in this shifting boundary between buildings and mobility vehicles, we should capture the context of the person as it travels with them. We should focus on humanizing the AI they will interact with as it contributes to their identity.

Sharing the data transparently will help train the AI to make it work for people will become important. This will give power to the designers and product managers to not only shape the experience of the user.

With the right AIX Design, we can ensure that buildings and vehicles are not vying for the person's attention but are expanding the definition of the city to include the buildings, vehicles, community of people who become part of people's mobility solution. In such a world, AIX Designers will empower people to shape their identities as mobile beings.

CHAPTER 16: OPEN DATA AND OPEN AI

16.1 What is Open AI?

Our minds should become open and unbiased to develop correct AI technologies. Our devices should share data openly to allow for the action of machines to share openly. The lack of interoperability among IoT devices today is not the same bias as in data but another form of bias limiting customers to one company's products, limiting open access to home or building data. Non-interoperability of devices creates silos of products. Biased data leads to silos of humans impacted by the incorrect AI models. In the end not being open either way fragments humanity and impacts servicing our customers to the full potential of possibilities promised by automating buildings with technology.

Open Datasets are available for every possible industry that your team can use to learn to train models. Companies are posting dataset in schema.org which is an open standard. Google moved their dataset search out of beta in Jan 2020. This allows you to search on any keyword to find datasets, many open, and some proprietary to companies on all possible topics globally.

Kaggle runs competitions covering several industries and typically partners with several players and gets the necessary datasets needed to train for its competitions. Kaggle has a large open dataset for sales conversion optimization that can be used to run clustering algorithms to segment customers. (Ref. https://www.kaggle.com/loveall/clicks-conversion-tracking)

16.2 Federated AI

Federated AI is a form of distributed Machine Learning done across multiple companies or groups. This is typically done in the Finance industry for companies to build upon each other's fraud models, to help their customers and reduce business risk. In Federated AI, each company does not share their customer data while working collaboratively with others. Energy industry uses Federated AI. The downside of Federated AI is that because it is a blackbox, without much interpretability, any error in one of the models can be propagated downstream to all partners working on the Federated AI model.

Still, in some industries companies cannot make progress by competing to solve the same problem. In 2019, Autonomous Vehicle technology companies realized this and started putting out their dataset for Car Cognition as open data. Only by collaborating and building a Federated AI will the car industry truly get to autonomous vehicles by 2030.

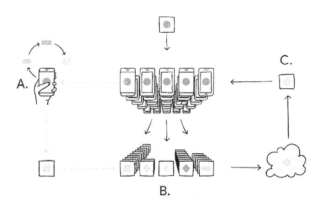

image: google

Driverlessworldschool.com   @sujamthe   27

16.3 Interpretability and Explainable AI

Machine Learning Interpretability is described by Prof Lakkaraju of Harvard Business School and Harvard HEAS as, "The ability to explain or to present in understandable terms to a human." Since all AI algorithms operate on statistical probability, they are never at 100% confidence levels. Explainable AI is a way for the algorithm to show transparently how it arrived at a certain prediction. This is prevalent in healthcare where even a 0.1% change in confidence can lead to a life and death decision. Explainable AI tries to show what data was used in creating the AI model that is influencing the prediction or decision.

CHAPTER 17: AI Ethics

AI Ethics has evolved to be a fast growing area of AI. As we discussed earlier, the data that trains AI is biased and reflects the biases of the humans collecting and organizing this training data. So the AI used in facial recognition algorithms ends up being biased towards some segments of the population, leading to more false positives. AI is automating some jobs and is affecting the lives of some people in negative ways. As we face the reality of climate change, AI can be a tool in the hands of ethicists for bringing about climate justice. AI is able to manipulate images and news, and create 'fake news' that spreads false information by manipulating social media data associated with people's behaviours and biases. AI data can compromise the privacy of some people and become a tool for data bullying in the hands of others.

So there is one school of thought with ethicists who believe that AI should be prevented from building systems that hurt and marginalize some people. They want to use regulation as a tool to stop unethical AI. The other school of thought shares the same truth and goals but believes that instead of regulating, we should focus on developing ethical AI, with openness and transparency of the underlying data that powers AI. Interpretability of AI and explainable AI can help create transparency.

Ethics in technology has become a critical conversation in governments and corporations alike. Companies are creating Ethics departments and guidelines. Universities have begun teaching ethics as part of technology education.

Mia Dand founded Women in AI Ethics (WIAE) and has developed it as a globally influential force to drive AI ethics in industry and the public sector with a growing group of women leaders, researchers and ethicists.

"Ethics in AI can't be an afterthought. It has to be part of the AI design process right from the start to ensure there are no ethical blindspots. - Mia Dand"

WIAE has developed AI Ethics frameworks for industry to develop ethics in AI as they go through digitization of companies and cities.

17.1 AI Ethics Framework

Women in AI Ethics is a global organization of hundreds of brilliant minds that is focused on bringing ethics into the central decision making process of working with AI. Their AI ethics framework is very comprehensive and addresses security, privacy, transparency, accountability, and adds sustainability and rights of people to inform the right decision making framework.

Figure: AI Ethics Framework from WAIE credit: Lighthouse3

17.2 Suing an algorithm?

2017 was just the start of the world getting automated with algorithms for everything from scheduling, to shopping to travel planning. In 2016, BMW shared a 'Next 100 Vision' with an Augmented Reality dashboard and 'companion' algorithm, stating that it "symbolizes the intelligence, connectivity and availability" of the car that can perform autonomous routine tasks or give advice to the driver.

This use of AI algorithms raises questions about who is in charge and who bears the risks? Companies build algorithms by feeding data to the programs. Ted Friedman of Gartner tweeted in 2016 saying, "With the rise of algorithmic business, data governance must address not only data quality but also the quality of algorithms."

What does it mean to have quality governance similar to data governance? Data about users often reveals more about our behavior than we want to share, invading our privacy and breaking compliance required in some industries such as insurance, healthcare, and online marketing.

Can a Poor Quality Algorithm Harm Us?

The algorithm can give us bad advice. With a self-driving car, it could make bad decisions and drive erratically. As long as it follows the government regulation to drive safely at Level 5 automation, we are still safe.

A bad algorithm may be a poorly written algorithm that breaks into our privacy. It could learn our habits and misuse that data. It could hold us hostage to a particular service by saving our friend's contacts. It could spam our friends in our name without our permission. It could sell our behavioral information to companies. It could offer to help us shop better, but favor the retailer or travel provider over the consumer. That is not just bad quality; that is outright dishonest business practice. All of this adds to the risk of the car, or the algorithmic business, and creates an unprecedented challenge for the insurance company.

So checking the quality of an algorithm seems to be about ensuring that the algorithm follows privacy and data usage policies that apply to humans, and to make sure its business model is one of honesty and integrity. It is about checking these for the people and firms that develop and control these algorithms.

Figure: Knightscope Security Robot in the Mall, San Jose

Credits: Sudha Jamthe

In the Westfield mall in San Jose, there is a security robot called Knightscope. It looks at the faces of people to track for security violations. Since a mall is a public space, we do not know what data is captured from people and kids, nor what uses it will be put to in the future. Without regulation, there is no transparency on what is captured and how it is interpreted or saved for future use. AIX designs the AI, the robot in this case. AIX will help keep the focus on users and ensure that the data is collected with the user's consent, providing an experience that will earn and retain the user's, assuring that user will help them with security.

17.3 Inequality & Climate Justice

Today, the world is facing more income inequality than ever before. Self-driving cars, by design, are reliant on the road infrastructure to train the software for the car to drive safely. So countries with poor infrastructure get left behind. This will motivate them to adopt drones faster than autonomous cars and trucks. Autonomous drones from Zipline offer medical delivery in war-torn Rwanda, and the drones from Matternet do freight delivery in rugged mountains of Nepal. After self-driving cars serve the metro population, they will improve their technology to run in rough terrains and adapt to poor infrastructure environments. They will also build out connected infrastructure, like connected pavement with sensors, so it is a 2-way innovation in which both sides will feed upon each other in developing countries.

Developing countries will also force the development of the technology to be more autonomous, requiring fewer trained personnel, low power consumption and easy set up by untrained professionals making it more user-friendly. It will also expedite the innovation with the focus on different problems. In Africa, the focus is not on traffic and commute, but on food equality and expanding the the electric grid from multi-family solar grids, to optimize green energy across a wider geography. This will lead to greater focus on autonomous freight delivery of food and smart trucks that keep food safe. It will result in autonomous vehicles that do Vehicle-to-Vehicle communication to share power when a critical autonomous vehicle carrying medicine loses power and another driving nearby can offer back-up.

In Nigeria, an entrepreneur, Angel Adelaja, is innovating to grow plants in shipping containers indoors. Like transportation, agriculture is one of the top industries to use sensors and data to optimize yield and to keep grain storage and transportation safe. Again, in countries that face drought, or in California and Australia where wildfires are becoming more prevalent, AI is being used to predict weather patterns, and computer vision is used to augment human intelligence with predictions on which plants to grow or weed out for an optimal yield.

Artificial Intelligence in such situations helps address inequality by creating equal opportunity for developing countries, while providing climate justice to areas hit harder by climate change beyond their control.

Again, the success of these implementations comes down to AIX. Generic AI models from Silicon Valley cannot solve Africa's problem. An AI model addressing drought in Indonesia needs data from Indonesia to solve local problems effectively. So AIX, designing with local data to build AI models that develop predictions and recommendations, will help solve local problems and help reduce the inequality that comes from climate change.

The same applies to the visually impaired. The self-driving car has driver-set Autopilot modes, which expect the driver to let the car run autonomously but watch and jump in if there is an emergency situation. Entrepreneurs can use sensors to create way finders for blind people in cities. My prediction is that we will build out self-driving cars for the visually impaired in the next decade, allowing for human interaction with the car using voice and Augmented Reality. This will make it a more natural, human-like interaction instead of a forced interaction with a computer. The car will identify users by biometrics and give them much needed mobility. AIX is needed to create this experience by designing for voice and AR to work for the visually impaired user.

Women in AI

The technology industry has long been considered more difficult for women, with published pay gaps for women among other things. Since AI works on data, having women contribute their perspective is important to get to an AI that will scale and work for all people. The good news is that women authors of AI research papers are increasing globally. Women are contributing more in the area of AI Ethics, with a sense of deep understanding of where AI research is headed.

Growth in female authorship of AI paper, 2000-18

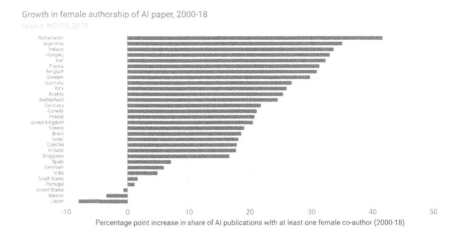

Percentage point increase in share of AI publications with at least one female co-author (2000-18)

Figure: Growth in Female AI Authorship from AI index 2019 report

17.3 Morality vs Ethics

Moral Machines

As our world becomes more autonomous with intelligent machines, it is important to be aware that we are putting autonomous decision-making in the hands of machines. Humans train these machines and give them the training data to build models to use when making decisions. They unknowingly include their biases in this data, essentially teaching the machines their own biases.

One classic problem debated among experts is called the "Trolley Problem," where a trolley has to decided to switch between two paths with both of them killing some number of people.

MIT set up a Moral Machines site (http://moralmachine.mit.edu/) where we can choose between two scenarios, each of which incorporates decisions made by a crashing self-driving car based on the knowledge of who will get killed. It is set up as a crowd-sourced site to collect human perspectives on moral decisions made by intelligent machines such as self-driving cars.

One business question to ask is whether a self-driving car company should expose its moral decision capabilities and how it will impact the customer's decision to choose their car over their competition. But there is no winning in this path. Will your customers buy a machine that has a high moral compass or will they shun buying a self-driving car that admits killing its passengers to save pedestrian lives? The same can be extended to moral decisions when using AI for highly sensitive situations, like using Robots or Drones. Or when AI gets programmed to make decisions in robotic surgery, or when making recommendations on when to call a doctor, or whether to take medicines for health conditions.

Such questions get raised as theoretical options, with our fear of letting go and giving control to an intelligent machine that will make decisions in all walks of life

Our changing relationship with Intelligent Machines

The question remains about our changing relationship with intelligent machines including invisible AI, voice assistants and self-driving vehicles.

Our experiences are nuanced and filtered by context, identity, and relevance based on location and time. This is influenced by our moods and biases that are stored deep in our lizard brains controlling how we feel, perceive reality, get creative, solve problems, define and store as memory. Our experiences, and our recall of those experiences shape our identity and help us grow in self-awareness. This underlying ability to live our experience as life is human intelligence. Add free will to it, and it creates many billion unique combinations, making it complicated to replicate the human experience and human cognition. So we thought.

As we get comfortable with autonomous vehicles driving us, it is not going to be a "thing" that is at our call to drive us around. Our dependence on intelligent machines, including our cars, will blur our sense of the reality of who is in-charge.

How will our relationship with the machine change as it smartens up, and begins to advise us? There is research currently being conducted on how our interaction with devices will change our behavior with other humans. Moving toward a more autonomous world will surely impact human interaction as much or more than any tech we have experienced in the past.

Affective computing teaches machines to understand emotions with the goal to develop empathy to help them fit in socially and to take actions based on sensing our emotions. Wize Mirror from Semeoticons, a project from the Italian National Research Council, measures a person's overall health from facial recognition. The AI promised in the "The Next 100 years" from BMW may very well do that, as well.

When our car reminds us to manage our temper, in our own self-interest, to help us maintain our own physical safety, we may be crossing that line where control shifts to the car. So I would advise that we put the human at the center of designing all forms of Artificial Intelligence. It is easy to look at everything as data when you build models. Start AIX with the human and the specific problem you are trying to solve, and then consider how far you would ethically go if you were on the receiving end of the AI's interaction. If you as a project manager are going to use voice to train a model to identify a person like Google Home, it is imperative to go into the future and look at what can be done with this data for voice as biometrics, and design your data collection, user consent and engagement experience ethically.

Figure: My IoT student, Amar Chhatwal, IoT Energy expert & Enterprise Operational & Strategy Leader.

Chapter 18: Ethical and Smart Automation

Companies are automating any job that can be broken down into repeatable steps. Some of these jobs are being replaced slowly and in some cases workers are expected to train the AI to take over their jobs.

Successful companies know that what makes them unique and sustainable in the market is not that they produce a particular product in scale with cost efficiencies. This might be the case in manufacturing similar parts on a small scale. We are in the knowledge economy with technology becoming an integral part of every company. What this means is that technology (not only AI) is being adopted by companies in every department to build better products and improve processes for quality, customer service, marketing, sales, shipping and keeping employees happy. HIstorically, technology gets adopted, not through a few repeat steps but through a digital transformation journey that occurs differently in each company. Innovative ideas that improve processes and products are crucial for technology to permeate established companies and fields. Employees do this by caring for customers, and by applying business acumen attained over time, understanding their products and services and the secret sauce that makes their particular company successful compared to competition in the same market.

Many companies scale and grow successfully because of the culture that is woven into the daily functioning of their employees.

When companies automate their products and processes using AI, this intrinsic knowledge that resides in companies needs to be captured. This cannot be done by breaking an employee's job down into steps that can train an AI to replace jobs. In manufacturing, many robots and robotic arms are replacing repeated jobs on workers. The jobs that are hazardous for humans and monotonous will be replaced in the long run. But the culture of the company and human business acumen can be lost and will hurt the company if the employees' jobs are automated as process automations.

AIX

Job Interviews by HireVue

Several large companies are using AI to filter candidates before they get called in for an interview. HireVue gets a video from candidates and offers filtering of candidates to companies offering analysis of people's personality to offer insights about cultural fit to companies.

In this case, AI is doing the screening that was previously done by recruiters. This raises questions about whether AI can inform the company of how it is making decisions on personality and the candidates' soft skills. It also raises the question of what perception these company brands give their candidates when they delegate their first point of contact with future hires to be an AI? This is a classic case where AIX design of the AI is needed for multiple stakeholders involved. An empathy mapping should be done to understand the needs of interview candidates, HR, hiring managers, and employees who make internal referrals. The correct human-computer interface should be built before just launching the AI as an algorithm that runs on its own to solve a problem.

CHAPTER 19: Conclusion

Here's to your success creating AI Business with AIX, harnessing the power of data to create AI Algorithms and iterating to arrive at an experience that is just right for your customer!!!

AI is pervasive. Across all industries. Affects all walks of life. AI promises a future where everything is connected to the Internet, data flows everywhere, diseases are stopped before they hurt us, cars driving us autonomously, planes running seamlessly, dams stopped before flooding and people given personalized shopping, entertainment, and education.

AI also creates fear that automation will eliminate jobs, and that it could lead to a police state where our every move is tracked and facial recognition tracks us in the city. Some people extrapolate a future where humans will have tiny devices swimming inside our bodies watching every cell for diseases, tracking our moods and biometrics, a brain cap tracking our thought as data to drive a wheelchair or track mental health and get help, getting us to the state of singularity where humans augment their intelligence with machines to become one with them.

The reality lies is the promise, waiting for you to harness it.

The reality is the limitation of narrow AI being created for specific problems. We will have to go a long way to taste the good before we get to the bad. AI Ethics and need for people of multiple fields to get involved to share the future gives me hope that we will harness AI technology with responsibility.

The reality is that all this data sits in silos in companies resisting change to their ways of doing business, waiting for designers to create the experiences customers want and need, for businesses to bear the risk of testing what business models work, for product managers to train the AI to shape it to products, services and solutions. As Aleksander Poniewiersky, author of "SPEED" says "Partnerships with data and AI are more intricate balance of power among the ecosystem of partners because the success comes from the partnership and no single person owns the success more than others (typically)." This means we are waiting for business development and market development leaders to figure out how to create, test and scale partnerships that involve trading data as the currency.

We are witnessing a historic moment in artificial intelligence creating new jobs and automating others, changing how we live in every industry and every walk of life. AI woken us as humans on a questioning of how we live, work, move and the fundamental definition of what it means to be sentient beings on earth and what is our role to co-exist or as masters of machines that we have created.

You as the AI researcher have the power to create the right model. You as the product manager and business person holds the power and responsibility to train the AI. Be a ruthless teacher and find out what the AI has learnt. Take it like a child hungry to learn to be told right from wrong. Expose it's biases.

You as a the AI Designer have the power and responsibility to design the right human computer interface using voice or computer vision. You hold the power to redefine our dependency on machines and whether we will dull our senses to give us free will in a world of machines.

I call you to harness the power of AI with creativity and responsibility. Look at the opportunity to not just solve problems for some people to create more consumption but for all people because as Joe Toscano says " AI is about automating humanity."

Look for opportunities to solve humanity's greatest problems - environmental threats, inequality from redefining jobs to what work means in an automated world, what new efficiency will delight you and your customers and move us forward on our journey as humanity.

Welcome to your career pivot to AIX to shape our worlds into the future.

Epilogue by Rob Van Kranenburg

We are at the beginning of another technological revolution. This shift is already happening. A June, 2016 Price, Waterhouse, Coopers report found electronic manufacturing services (EMS) companies offering new services moving into, "new models of joint design manufacturing and outsourced design manufacturing." When asked, "What Is the Biggest Challenge Facing the Manufacturing Industry Today?" in the 2017 Industry Week Salary Survey, 21-29 year olds replied, "balancing the roles of machine and human interaction in intelligent manufacturing environments." As you can see from Sudha Jamthe's work, this trend is not limited to manufacturing.

Very few companies are foreshadowing the trends, but it is not a surprise that one of the most interesting ones stems from a background combining interest in how machines learn (deep learning) and how people learn. Landing.AI is a Silicon Valley startup founded by Andrew Ng, who supervised the development of Stanford University's main MOOC (Massive Open Online Courses) platform. When people question if AI can take over humans, Andrew Ng has said that fearing a rise of killer robots is like worrying about overpopulation on Mars.

According to a recent Zinnov report, The Spring of AI: Leveraging Collective Disruptor Insights, the US is the dominant innovation hotbed for AI start-ups led by the Bay Area, building an AI-first future with, "$10B in acquisitions, 300+ patents and 30K AI talent." According to the report the main reasons for AI startup failures are regulatory restrictions, business models and product market (non) fits. Europe is leading the world in regulating data and AI while keeping balance on innovation on people's privacy and consent.

The hardest concept to grasp in this Digital Transition is the relative (semi) autonomous gaze of the network itself. This network is a balance of cloud and edge services (data storage on the device), with AI running inside objects in everyday activities (wearables, washing machines, cars). For this network all its users are 'entities': machines, people and processes (templates that predefined scenarios).

This is also the message of this book: the AI strategy should address these issues at operational as well as strategic levels as well as building an ecosystem at the lowest possible level of materiality between the companies themselves and their ecosystems.

Acknowledgments

I am thankful to my Mom - my No.1 cheerleader who makes me feel that the world is limitless, every single day. My daughter Neha Jamthe, you stop me from tailgating self-driving cars reminding me that there is a real person ready to take over, reminding me of the fragile balance between AI and humans. You are the rock that grounds me and my light that keeps me going. I am humbled and blessed to be your Mom.

Dr. Charles Ikem, AI Designer and Service Designer from Italy who was bold enough to join me to explore and create the world of AIX with my "AIX" online course on DriverlessWorldSchool. Your live YouTube conversations have been an inspiration for me to get into the crowded world of AI, armed with my love of data, to stop and think about AI as the language with humans and how to design end to end AI.

Thank You to so many of my Stanford students and readers for discussions, questions and inspiration about the future of tech, IoT and AI.

Richard Meyers, my editor, for your relentless pursuit to make me communicate better, improve my writing to make this a better book than any of my past work. I am thankful for when you walked in as my Stanford student to my Internet of Things Business course and offered to edit my book one day. Finally, we managed to work together. Your endless curiosity and patience in challenging my thinking about the many paths to the future with Artificial Intelligence has made me smarter. Thank You Tamara McCleary for sharing the AI journey and writing the foreword.

I am so blessed to have many people who believe in me and cheer me on, as I embark on each new crazy project. You make me fly, making me believe that the world is limitless.

AJit Joakar of Oxford University, you showed me what was possible with AI and Deep Learning and gave me a new lens to look at IoT and data with Computer Vision and Facial recognition four years back. You challenged me to bring more technical depth to my case studies as I strive to address the business dimension of AI modelling.

To Rob Van Kranenburg of EU IoT Council who gave me pointers and engaged me through my discovery of Cognitive IoT and the regulations and communications of a Driverless car. Thank You Sally

A. Applin and Michael D. Fisher from the University of Kent for your research about multiple communications in Automobiles as pioneers in 2012. Thank You, Ken Herron for your trust in my abilities and for sharing your and Toby Ruckert's work from UIB to inspire me to think about new ways machines can communicate with humans. The Bosch camera, powered by Unified Inbox, that can chat using Whatsapp to report about lines in airport coffee shops, inspired me to delve deeper into the AIX power of Computer Vision. Thank you to Oluwatobi Oyinlola and Josep Clotet Soler for inspiring me everyday.

Prof. Rosalind W. Picard of MIT, you don't know me, but your work on Affective computing is my inspiration and I hope that we can get the Driverless car to communicate with the human driver one day.

Patrick Slavenberg, thank you for your many brainstorms about AI models and your contribution of the personalization case study and many reviews of AI Algorithms. Christian Mastradonato for introducing me to the power or AR in the enterprise, Jane Ren for the power of Digital Twins, Sebastián García Marra and Dalton Oliveira, Flávio Maeda for showing me power of IIoT in LATAM, Ricardo Baeza-Yates thank you for your inspiration and love of data. Thank You.

Mia Dand, thank you for picking up the leadership mantle to stop and challenge that AI needs to be built ethically and creating the Women in AI Ethics to bring 100s of powerful, intelligent AI women. You are an inspiration with your global AI Ethics framework and regional chapters to hold the world accountable to build AI to serve us all ethically.

All AI industry experts who shared case studies to enrich the learning of my students, to understand the corporate best practices of building AI solutions, you got my book grounded in reality while not losing focus on futuristic possibilities with AI. Jeff Fryer of Arm from Austin, US, Vinay Manglani, Kishor Kulkarni and Dr. Omkar Gurjar of VigourSoft from India, Alex D'Elia from Italy, David kerrigan from Ireland, Dalton Oliveira from Brazil, Patrick Slavenburg from Netherlands, Ken Herron and UIB team from Singapore and Aleksander Poniewierski and EY team from Poland. Robert Schwentker, my friend, you keep me inspired about Blockchain and Open AI. Thank You.

Every one of my readers, students and conference keynote attendees, my WeeklyWed Live YouTube users, you keep challenging me and keep me in a learning mode, and many times grounding me to the global reality of building AI solutions across different industries, different customer cultures and different data sensitivities and regulations. Thank You.

Thank You Roxy for joining me on my crazy plan to interview IoT Women from around the globe for IoT Day, April 9th. Your brilliance with data and focus with customers keeps me grounded. I am thankful to the amazing women in IoT and AI that we have interviewed, drawn inspiration from and learnt from - Tejumade Afonja who ran AI Saturdays in Lagos, Nigeria and is now a Grad students at Universität des Saarlandes, Saarbrücken, Germany, Aarthi Srinivasan of Amazon AWS, Annie Reddaway from London, and Manon Den Dunnen of Netherlands and many more that I cannot list everyone here, you know who you are!

Marsha Collier and Brian Solis, you are my role models of where I want to be as an author. I hope to make you proud with each new book. Thank you.

And to my AI admin Amy, from x.ai, thank you for keeping me productive and teaching me the reality of how hard you work to interact with humans and our unpredictable ways.

To you my reader! You have trusted me and have begun this journey with me. I am here only because of You! Thank You!

About The Author

Sudha Jamthe is the CEO of IoTDisruptions.com and a globally recognized Technology Futurist, with a 20+ year mix of entrepreneurial, academic and operational experience. Sudha loves shaping new technology ecosystems and mentoring business leaders on digital global transformation strategies. Her first passion is to help her students who inspire her and are set to create the future connected, autonomous, driverless world.

She is the author of three IoT books, "IoT Disruption", "The Internet of Things Business Primer" and "IoT Disruptions 2020" and one book on Autonomous Vehicles "2030 The Driverless World". Her specialty is business model evolutions and business innovators from data. Sudha teaches "Autonomous Vehicle Business" and "Artificial Intelligence Bootcamp " courses at Stanford Continuing Studies

Program. She hosts "The IoT Show" and a Weekly Wed Live Q&A on YouTube, to bring global practitioners together to share best practices in IoT, AI and Autonomous Vehicles space.

Sudha is a champion for STEM programs and Girls Who Code. Earlier, she served as a venture mentor at MIT and Director of Bay Area Facebook, Twitter, Pinterest and Google+ Meetups and served as a member of (P007) IEEE global initiative on ethical considerations on the fail-safe development of autonomous and intelligent systems. She actively contributes to TechCrunch, Mashable, Venturebeat, Huffington Post, Automated Buildings and TechTarget and Axios as a respected technology futurist. She is the chair of the strategic advisory board of Barcelona Technology School, developing digital transformation leaders, on the Advisory to Dean College of Engineering, Northwestern Polytechnic University, a proud member of the EU IOT Council, and ambassador to FundingBox Impact Connected Car Europe.

You can reach her at http:// sudhajamthe.com or @sujamthe on Twitter.

Praise For Sudha Jamthe's IoT Books

"Sudha Jamthe's no-nonsense approach to IoT is refreshing, informative, and thorough. Read ``The Internet of Things Business Primer if you want to succeed in the IoT ecosystem." - **Ben Parr, Author of *Captivology*, CEO of Co-founder/CMO Octane AI & one of Inc.'s Top 10 IoT Experts**

Sudha brings case studies from IoT Entrepreneurs and Product Builders globally and combines it with in-depth analysis from her own experience with Mobile Products to offer a must-read book about how to build a successful IoT Business. Watch out this is one of those books you are going to read and reread many times to serve as your bible as the IoT ecosystem shapes out over the next few years."- **Myles Weissleder SF NewTech Meetup Founder**

"The Internet of Things Business Primer" is a guidebook for innovators, entrepreneurs and technology leaders looking for practical examples of best practices to build a successful IoT business. Sudha brings her own experience and the one of other entrepreneurs that have had a meaningful impact on charting the path of the IoT industry" - **Davide Vigano, CEO Sensoria Inc.**

"Analysis of IoT from a business perspective by a seasoned business and product leader – that is what this book is all about. Sudha has done an amazing job in evaluating IoT and has shown us how to make a business out of it. This is not an easy task and Sudha has done complete justice to it." - **Pragati Rai Sr Innovation specialist Deutsche Bank & Author Android Application Security Essentials**

"Sudha is an amazing thought leader in the new and exciting field of IoT. She is talented and inspiring with her words and work. It's exciting to see her put her deep knowledge of IoT and sharp vision of the future of this trend of technology into this book" - **Ahmed Banafa, Professor San Jose State University**

" We live in a connected world that continues to evolve each day. And therein lies the opportunity to build a business. Sudha Jamthe brings her years of experience as a technologist to this comprehensive guide, applying her own experience, and drawing from others in case studies that solidify important concepts. *The Internet of Things Business Primer* is the definitive source for anyone looking to blaze a path in the IoT world and be successful doing it." -

Frank Gruber CEO and Cofounder of Tech.co and Author Startup Mixology

"Sudha Jamthe's new book provides the definitive roadmap for building an IoT business and navigating the forthcoming disruption across many industries with a comprehensive overview covering technology, business models and use cases" - **Ajit Jaokar Author of Data Science for IoT and CEO Futuretext.**

"I really enjoyed Sudha's first book "IoT Disruptions" that covers the universe of opportunities that IoT is bringing to our lives. This book "The Internet of Things Business Primer" goes deeper to offer an in-depth guide and case studies for anyone who wants to learn how to build an IoT Business to accelerate the digital transformation."- **Josep Clotet, Founding Managing Director, Barcelona Technology School**

"Sudha is a great supporter of the grassroots of Silicon Valley. I had the honor to work with her, when developing Startup Weekend back in 2010 with eBay and PayPal. In this book Sudha is leveraging her unique insight to prepare the next wave of innovation and support the IoT community. This is not another book about IoT, this is a map on how to navigate the future of IoT entrepreneurship." -

Franck Nouyrigat. Co-founder Global Startup Weekend and Partner recorp

'I have known Sudha for many years and she is highly respected for her insights in developing products for the 21st century. She really is a visionary, able to spot new technology trends in the social and mobile arenas. Read this book, slowly and digest her advice. I suspect you will refer back to it many times' **- Brian Solis, Principal Analyst, Altimeter Group, a Prophet company.**

Appendix 1: AI Algorithms for the DataScience Team

(Thank You Patrick Slavenburg for your contribution to this list)

Correlation is a basic statistics model that shows the relation between two variables.

Error is the confidence interval of how accurate the prediction is. It is important for the business person to know the error or confidence interval of an algorithm. For example, would you trust an AI that predicts that a patient has cancer with 99% confidence or one with 70% confidence.

Inference Model is the software that carries the AI model and is ready to look at a piece of data be it a number or an image such a person's face and make a prediction or decision for which it has been trained in its algorithm.

Algorithm: Linear Regression

Linear Regression: Regression tries to fit the best line of the data to predict the value of a random variable based on known fixed variable. Regression line is also called 'sum of squares errors'. The basic form of linear regression tries to minimize the sum of the squared deviation predictions.

Algorithm: Logistic Regression

Logistic regression uses a "logistic function" to differentiate between usually 2 classes. Tumor: Yes/No. Pass/Fail. Loyal Customer/Not loyal customer. Healthy/Sick. Etc.

Algorithm: Linear Regression using **Gr**adient Descent
It is a variation of linear regression. It uses gradient descent optimization to fit the line to reduce the error and increase confidence of the AI model.

Algorithm: Linear **D**iscriminant Analysis

Algorithm: **C**lassification
A classification algorithm predicts in which class a particular event falls. E.g. Based on the pixels in an X-Ray the algorithm decides if a particular "blob" is a tumor or not. The classes in this case are: Yes (a tumor), No (not a tumor). In customer segmentation in marketing there can be many classes. Starbucks for example uses 100,000+ classes for their email newsletter. With every new customer a classification algorithm decides in which of those 100K classes this customer falls. Based on that result the person will receive a personalized newsletter.

Algorithm: **Decision** Trees
Decision trees are a graphical representation of all the possible solutions to a decision.

Algorithm: **N**aive Bayes
Algorithm: **K**-Nearest Neighbors

Algorithm: Learning Vector Quantization

Algorithm: **S**upport Vector Machines (SVM)

Algorithm: Bagged **D**ecision Tree
Algorithm: **R**andom Forest
Algorithm: **B**oosting and AdaBoost

Appendix 2: Best practice mapping data to AI models (from experts on researchgate & quora)

1. Tradeoff between accuracy and generalisation. The more
   accurate your classifier is on your training data, the less it
   will probably generalise (depends on your training data). This
   is called overfitting and cross validation tries to avoid that.
   This is why you mix training and test data on each fold.
   (Credit: Efstathios Branikas, University of Strathclyde)

2. Do you need a neural network for a prediction problem?
   (Credit: Pavel Kordík, Czech Technical University in Prague |
   ČVUT · Faculty Information Technology (FIT))
   If you have a classification problem, use a weak learner such
   as Linear regression or Logistic regression then scale to
   neural network and increase the nodes. Use Rapidminer and
   setup an experiment to measure generalization
   performance (average test error) of several algorithms.

3. How do you decide how many hidden layers and how many nodes to add to hidden nodes in a neural network? (Prediction network)

Underfitting = too few neurons to detect signals in the complicated data set.

Overfitting = too many neurons

Ans: Use a heuristic method such as cross-validation to test accuracy of the test set by dividing the data into training set and validation or test set. Low number of nodes will allow the network to generalize. Too many nodes will allow the AI to recall the training set to perfection.

More layers used for difficult problems like facial recognition, handwritten character recognition.

"you can find the number of layer and neurons by using the global optimization algorithm such as particle swarm, simulated annealing, patternsearch, bayesian optimization, and etc, to minimize the validation errors"

(Credit: Inhyeok Yim, Gwangju Institute of Science and Technology)

4. Classification (Credit: Mohammad Norizadeh Cherloo, Iran University of Science and Technology)

In pattern recognition we classify input data regarding its feature vector.in classification problems we have feature space that can be linear or nonlinear. These feature vectors for each input data determines which part of feature space it is located. In linear feature space datasets are linearly separated so we can simply find the line between 2 classes and then it can be used for classification of new datasets. In non-linear space the datasets are non-linearly separate and it's complicated! Here's what we do in this case. According to the covers theorem, when we have non-linear space, we can simply map a nonlinear data into linear space using a non-linear kernel, so in this new feature space samples become linearly separated! And then again we simply find a separating line in new linear feature space. Non-linear svm uses this theorem for non-linear data.

Appendix 3: List of AIX Case Studies

1. Blockchain for Energy Consumption

2. Chatbot for Carrier's Customer Support

3. AI based Quality Control of Oil Refinery

4. Digital Transformation of Smart Building

5. McDonald's Personalized Menu at drive-thru

6. AI in Healthcare - Listening out for us

7. Omnichannel Personalization for Retail

8. Low cost ARM solution for Computer Vision AI

9. Automated Building Management

10. Retail Ad platform

Appendix 4: AI Research & References

Statistics Reference

PwC's Artificial Intelligence Study estimates AI market size at $15.7 Trillion to Global Economy by 2030

https://www.pwc.com/gx/en/issues/data-and-analytics/publications/artificial-intelligence-study.html

Warehouses in America https://www.bls.gov/iag/tgs/iag493.htm

AI In the Car

https://www.forbes.com/sites/lianeyvkoff/2020/01/22/audi-trialing-v2x-to-warn-drivers-of-workers-on-the-highway/?ss=logistics-transport#7fd5f93348af

Driverless Cognitive AI Research References

'Parallel autonomy and autonomous cars, CSAIL-Toyota joint research effort'. By Javier Alonso-Mora, (MIT Computer Science and Artificial Intelligence Lab CSAIL)

MIT Prof Picards' work on Affective Deep Learning http://web.media.mit.edu/~picard/research.php

SAIL- Toyota AI research at Stanford http://aicenter.stanford.edu

Safe Feedback Interactions in Human-Autonomous Vehicle Systems

SUDHA JAMTHE

http://aicenter.stanford.edu/safe-feedback-interactions-in-human-autonomous-vehicle-systems/

AI in Automated Buildings

Ken Sinclair Interview with Sudha Jamthe about designing for shared spaces. https://youtu.be/Fn8vHrCiIK4

Global AI Readiness Index

Global AI Vibrancy Tool - vibrancy.aiindex.org - an interactive tool that compares countries across 34 indicators

KPMG Autonomous Vehicles Readiness Index https://www.pwc.com/gx/en/issues/data-and-analytics/publications/artificial-intelligence-study.html#explorer

Oxford's Government AI readiness index https://www.oxfordinsights.com/ai-readiness2019 ts.com/ai-readiness2019

Tracking Open data of Governments https://index.okfn.org/

AI for Social Good by McKinsey Institute https://www.mckinsey.com/featured-insights/artificial-intelligence/applying-artificial-intelligence-for-social-good

Energy Forecast competition

AIX

https://en.wikipedia.org/wiki/Global_Energy_Forecasting_Competit
ion

Explainable AI

https://www.computerweekly.com/news/252476410/AI-skills-and-
explainable-data-models-are-top-concerns-for-2020

Autonomous Vehicles

Automotive company plans on releasing a self-driving car stats

https://www.statista.com/chart/7009/self-driving-cars-are-on-their-
way/

Lutz Pathfinder

https://www.autoblog.com/2015/02/12/the-lutz-pathfinder-pod-uk
-first-driverless-car-video/

GATEway

https://gateway-project.org.uk/the-gateway-project-announces-the
-next-phase-of-driverless-pod-trials/

Roboat in Amsterdam http://senseable.mit.edu/roboat/

Tesla Model S Autopilot Forward Collision Warning at Work

http://www.businessinsider.com/tesla-avoids-accident-before-happ
ens-2016-12

How Tesla Auto Pilot Works

http://www.whatafuture.com/2014/06/14/google-driverless-car-th
e-obstacle-detection-unit/

Shirish Jamthe's Open source Github on Self-driving car computer vision and Deep Learning models https://github.com/sjamthe/

Waleed Abdulla's Open source Github on Traffic Sign recognition with TensorFlow. His github has other CNN and Deep Learning work. https://github.com/waleedka/traffic-signs-tensorflow

Facial Recognition

Clearview AI scrapping faces from social networks to sell facial recognition to law enforcement https://www.forbes.com/sites/kateoflahertyuk/2020/01/26/clearview-ais-database-has-amassed-3-billion-photos-this-is-how-if-you-want-yours-deleted-you-have-to-opt-out/#5923d00460aa

Business models

Dominoes tests pizza delivery with self-driving cars http://money.cnn.com/2017/09/01/technology/future/free-transportation-self-driving-cars/index.html

Transportation Innovations

T-pods from Einride

AIX

http://mashable.com/2017/07/06/einride-self-driving-truck-t-pod-reveal/#LpmMPb98Qgqx

Moral Machines

MIT's Moral Machines' survey - http://moralmachine.mit.edu/

Artificial Intelligence and Futuristic Healthcare Technology

http://www.theguardian.com/technology/2014/dec/09/synapse-ibm-neural-computing-chip

http://amitsheth.blogspot.com/2015/03/smart-iot-iot-as-human-agent-human.html

Stanford One Hundred Year study on AI

https://ai100.stanford.edu/2016-report

http://hackaday.com/2017/01/12/at-last-an-open-source-electric-vehicle-from-a-major-manufacturer/

http://press.renault.co.uk/press-release/fb984a0e-7b5e-4f09-9c17-02fb185bd49d

http://www.inc.com/kevin-j-ryan/how-tesla-is-using-ai-to-make-self-driving-cars-smarter.html http://www.reuters.tv/v/Its/2017/01/08/a-web-of-self-driving-tech-alliances-build-up

Semeoticons, a facial recognition project from the Italian National Research Council http://www.semeoticons.eu/?page_id=577

Honda Co-operative Mobility Ecosystem

http://www.multivu.com/players/English/7988331-honda-ces-cooperative-mobility-ecosystem/

http://www.ibm.com/cognitive/advantage-reports/

AI Job interviews

https://www.cnn.com/2020/01/15/tech/ai-job-interview/index.html

Arm case study of TensorFlow Image Recognition ComputerVision Demonstration

https://www.svds.com/tensorflow-image-recognition-raspberry-pi/

Ethics Narrative Timeline

https://drive.google.com/drive/folders/1pcescctIFZLCm4RwF1OnLqVDlPCKB2tk

Recommendation Algorithms

Xavier Amatriain now co-founder and CTO of Curai Explainable AI startup built the AI recommendation model at Netflix. This video

AIX

below is his lecture to Machine Learning Summer School 2014 in Pittsburgh (full set of all Machine Learning lectures are a good resource for ML beginners http://www.mlss2014.com)
https://www.youtube.com/watch?time_continue=7&v=bLhq63ygoU8&feature=emb_logo

AI Ethics
Algorithmic Colonization by Abeba Birhane
https://slideslive.com/38922346/invited-talk-algorithmic-colonization
"Ethics is about Power" by Khari Johnson
https://venturebeat.com/2019/11/11/ai-ethics-is-all-about-power/
Google Dataset search https://datasetsearch.research.google.com/

Axon police body cam maker has decided not to add facial recognition to its business citing ethical issues
https://qz.com/1654630/axon-the-maker-of-police-body-cams-wont-pursue-facial-recognition/

Made in the USA
Las Vegas, NV
14 April 2023

70595836R00164